INSTANT

ARCHITECTURE

Merry Christmas Luke
1997 — Dad

INSTANT

ARCHITECTURE

BY ELEANOR LYNN NESMITH

A Byron Preiss Book

FAWCETT COLUMBINE • NEW YORK

Copyright © 1995 by Byron Preiss Visual Publications, Inc.

Cartoon Bank Credits: Michael Crawford © 1995—5, 140, 220. John Jonik © 1995—183. Mick Stevens © 1995—89.

The Cartoon Bank, Inc., located in Yonkers, NY, is a computerized archive featuring the work of over fifty of the country's top cartoonists.

Illustration Credits: © Archive Holdings—6, 9, 27, 31, 32, 53, 56, 58, 61, 63, 70, 72, 79, 80, 82, 91, 99, 107, 109, 121, 124, 125, 134, 138, 143, 151, 156, 158, 160, 161, 163, 164, 166, 169, 180, 182, 200, 201. © Esto Photographic: Ezra Stoller—195, 205, 225, 230. Scott Frances—195. Peter Aaron—213, 224, Jock Pottle—219, Tim Street-Porter—231. © Estro/Arcaid: Richard Bryant—217. Courtesy of the Art Institute of Chicago—173, 189, 192. Courtesy of the British Tourist Authority—111, 123, 127, 148. Courtesy of the French Government Tourist Offic—120, 139. Courtesy of the Greek National Tourist Organization—36, 40, 41, 43, 44. Courtesy of the Tourist Office of Spain—167. Coutesy of VSBA: Rollin R. La France—209. Courtesy of Eureka Springs—227. Coutesy of Seaside—218. Courtesy of Ohio State University—234.

All rights reserved under International and Pan-American Copyright Conventions. Published in the United States by Ballantine Books, a division of Random House, Inc., New York, and simultaneously in Canada by Random House of Canada Limited, Toronto.

Library of Congress Catalog Card Number: 94-90823

ISBN: 0-449-90699-X

Cover design by Heidi North

Manufactured in the United States of America

First Edition: August 1995

10 9 8 7 6 5 4 3 2

CONTENTS

ACKNOWLEDGMENTS

Lots of people helped to make this book happen, although I actually did all the really hard work, liking writing.

First, I should thank Michael Sagalyn at Byron Preiss Visual Publications for asking me to write *Instant Architecture*. Who would have thought that a serious design critic would be willing to make light of her livelihood? Next, kudos to Debbie Dee. If not for her ever-so-gentle professional push, I'll still be churning out that boring brand of copy she so dearly loved to publish.

I did get a lot of help along the way when it came to editing (and remembering deadlines). Jared Keiling was great. He's the kind of editor every writer dreams of. He knows his place is to rid my text of nasty things like dangling prepositions, not rewrite my words. Dinah Dunn at BPVP is another rare jewel in the world of publishing—she's actually nice and was very helpful. And Heather Moehn, who took care of all the last details.

I'd also like to thank my father and my friends who listened to a litany of complaints about this project. It would be impossible to list everybody, but I've got to credit Lee, Tom, Mike, Allen, Andrea, Amy, Ellen, Kathi, Margee, Robin, Carolyn, Dave, and Nancy. There's also Mark and Paul, they really didn't help much but I know they'd be hurt if I didn't mention them. In addition, I'm appreciative to the Capital City Reading Group for naming *Instant Architecture* their book of the month selection.

And of course, there are all those egotistical architects throughout the ages who made this treatise possible and the telling of the tale significantly less tiring.

INTRODUCTION

It's Friday night and you're in the mood for a *real* book. Your soul is crying out for a work of substance—a book that will satisfy your deep craving for knowledge. Then suddenly you remember your dreams of becoming an architect. During story hour as a kid, you paid attention to the construction techniques of the houses in the "Three Little Pigs." You preferred drawing floor plans of houses over doing your spelling homework. Your dream tree house had skylights, Doric columns and elevators. When everybody else was crafting tie racks in shop, you built a replica of Frank Lloyd Wright's "Mile-High Tower."

Somehow the next thing you knew you found yourself pursuing another professional calling—doctor, lawyer, or carnival worker. Not to worry, your vocational path might have digressed, but that doesn't mean you can't be accomplished about a subject that's close to your heart.

You head down to the local "artsy-fartsy" bookstore and scan the architecture section. There are lots of big glossy monographs on architects you've never heard of. You can't find a single book with a dust jacket depicting something that even remotely resembles a building. You consider yourself avant-garde, so you pick out three expensive books sporting covers that look like colliding planes of steel and glass.

Two months later the coffee-table books are still occupying the same prominent spot on your coffee table, where you deposited them, unread. It's not that you didn't try. You can't help it if you got bogged down in the latent neosuprematism, tactile palette of materials, the dynamic plasticity of the initial parti, cacophonous disjunctive, volumetrical fluidity, taxonomic-spatial elision, and fragmentary esthetics.

But you remind yourself that you do like architecture, with a capital A. Didn't you just read from cover to cover *Architectural Digest*'s L.A. issue on the houses of the stars? But you felt a little cheap in the morning when you realized the magazine was still spread open to a big glossy color photograph of Madonna's (or was it Marilyn Monroe's?) bedroom.

We Can Tell:
Instant Architecture Is Designed for You

Now you can put aside those fluffy shelter magazines, as well as those pretentious primers. It's time for *Instant Architecture*, a readable survey of the history of architecture. It covers all the bases, not just the landmark buildings of white kings and popes in Europe. Starting with ancient Egypt, *Instant Architecture* explores the design and engineering marvels throughout history, and places important buildings in their social context. The book concludes with the confused state of architecture today, where any *ism* goes.

Throughout history the built environment has been the badge of civilization. A lasting architecture is concrete proof of a society's accomplishments and contributions. Written histories can embellish the truth, but buildings rarely lie. A study of a society's structures provides a portrait of its culture and comforts, and an understanding of the history of architecture can provide insight into the continuous processes that have shaped the political history of the world.

Instant Architecture will help you come to understand what Winston Churchill meant when he said, "We shape our buildings, and afterwards our buildings shape us." (From his girth, one wonders what kind of rotunda he was reared in.)

HERE'S WHERE CORNERSTONE GETS LAID

More than merely a guidebook or a stylebook, *Instant Architecture* will tell you where and when certain developments first arose. You'll learn how spatial advances in architecture have always developed through structural innovations. First the ancient Egyptians mastered the simple post-and-lintel construction. Then the Greeks refined these basic building blocks to design temples that expressed their ideas of beauty and sense of order. The more pragmatic Romans took the Classical style and added sophisticated engineering to many great cities and impressive public works projects. In the Middle Ages, the Church showed who was boss through magnificent cathedrals that reached for the sky. In Chicago in the late nineteenth century, a rising American merchant class, with the help of steel structures and elevators, reached for the heavens but with fewer spiritual aspirations.

The book also describes how generations of architects built on these foundations of their forefathers. For example, some of the original Renaissance men went out and personally measured the landmarks of antiquity. With these figures and the writings of a Vitruvius (a first-century B.C. architectural historian), guys like Brunelleschi developed their own treatises on design that became the basis for much of Renaissance architecture.

Other architects *literally* built on past foundation, as in the case of the Louvre, which has been modified, enlarged, and adapted scores of times over nearly four hundred years. Still others use "foundations," sometimes from thousands of miles away, more figuratively. Look at the way architect I. M. Pei recently augmented that same Paris landmark—the Louvre—with a glazed pyramid that echoes forms from antiquity while managing to look unabashedly Modern.

HOW THIS BOOK IS ORGANIZED

Instant Architecture is presented in roughly chronological sequence and organized by the important "styles," as definable as that can be. Breaks in sequence happen when the book switches to "Eastern Asia" or "Mesoamerica," each of which developed a unique approach to design pretty much independent of developments on the European Continent. However, it would be impossible to encapsulate the complete history of architecture in a few hundred pages. So the buildings shown here were chosen to illustrate the main characteristics of a movement. And our choices are usually one of several you'll be able to recognize when you've read this book. There might be other famous edifices (like your personal favorite of a style, or the place where you fell in love on your last European holiday) that are not included and probably could have been substituted. C'est la vie!

In each chapter you'll get a pithy portrait of the period with a listing of the most important buildings; a concise glossary of architectural terms; the background on the social issues that shaped the civilization's built environment; and lucid descriptions of the esthetics and techniques of building. These details are tied together with analysis and chapter summaries. In addition, a variety of lighthearted sidebars embellish the solid information.

Because the book spans thousands of years and the entire globe, you will come away enriched, with an overview of the salient forms and functions of the great landmarks of all time. Finally, you will have more than enough anecdotes to let you star at the next cocktail party when the conversation turns to the art of architecture or the personalities of its leading patrons and practitioners. And if you get rich overnight and have the chance to endow a huge new building, we'll all be glad you read *Instant Architecture* first.

CHAPTER 1

ANCIENT EGYPT
(3200 B.C.–A.D. 100)

YOU MUST REMEMBER THIS

Of the ancient civilizations, we know more about the Egyptian than any other. The Egyptians left some great papyrus tomes, but the designs of their temples, tombs, and pyramids, with all those funny hieroglyphs, tell the real story of the people who lived along the Nile.

MOST FAMOUS FOR

Buildings that are standing after nearly five thousand years— and mummies still call them home:

★ Pyramids of Giza—Cheops, Chephren, and Mykerinos (2680–2490 B.C.)
★ Great Sphinx (around 2600 B.C.)
★ Great Temple of Amon, Karnak, Thebes (1530–323 B.C.)
★ Temple at Luxor, Thebes (1408–1300 B.C.)

A River Runs Through It

It's no wonder that Egypt is called "the gift of the Nile," the name with which the Greek historian Herodotus anointed this ancient civilization. Like a liquid information highway, the Nile—the world's longest river—extends 4,160 miles south into the African Continent. It is temperate and navigable, but was subject to unfailingly regular and benign flooding until the construction of the Aswan Dam in 1968.

Unlike the Mississippi River's flooding, which wreaks havoc every fourscore years or so, the Nile's annual overflowing historically made the region livable, if not downright cultivated. Every July to October for thousands of years, the Nile rose to inundate its low-lying banks with the rich black silt of the river. This fertile swath, 8 to 10 miles wide and extending 500 miles southward from its delta, is what we consider ancient Egypt. These habitable lands were flanked with shelves of rugged cliffs, beyond which lay an arid desert plateau. The great Egyptian society encompassed a land mass smaller than the State of West Virginia, and in comparison to that region's cultural finesse, we see just how far civilization has come in 5,000 years.

From Power Trip to Eternity

Egyptian history acknowledges thirty dynasties, the first beginning in 3200 B.C. It is difficult to comprehend the political and religious clout of their pharaohs. There isn't a pope or king or dictator who holds a handle to these egomaniacal rulers. Forget sanctioned doctrines awarding the divine rights of kings. In Egypt, a pharaoh was considered, by himself (they were men, except for Queen Hatshepsut) and by his subjects, an actual deity.

Accordingly, these old men-gods never died, they just relocated to an elaborate tomb to while away eternity. This philosophy created Egypt's two predominant types of monumental buildings: the enduring tomb pyramid, and the mysterious, solemn temple.

A 30-SECOND COURSE IN BLUEPRINTS

When you sing you begin with Do, Re, Mi; when you design you begin with Plan, Section, and Elevation.

Plan: A diagram of the layout of the building as viewed from above (can be the ground floor, an upper floor, or even the basement).

Section: An imaginary vertical slice *through* a building.

Elevation: The vertical face of the building—drawn either from the outside looking in or vice versa.

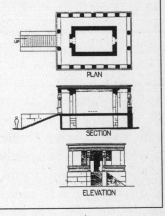

PLAN

SECTION

ELEVATION

DIDN'T THEY EVER DUST?

From the earliest signs of their having a distinct civilization, Egyptians were obsessed with the preservation and provisioning of their corpses. An incredible amount of energy and ingenuity was devoted to create a "homey" environment where the dead body would be as comfortable as possible for everlasting life. And for the pharaohs, the society spared nothing to that end.

As early as the First Dynasty, bands of linen were used to wrap the limbs of a royal body. Friends and family would provide a stash of the finest of earthly commodities so the corpse could continue to function comfortably forever. Not to worry about the old saying, "you can't take it with you," because in their minds these mummies weren't going anywhere. Based on the loot stashed in their tombs, Egypt probably spent about the same percentage of their GNP on taking care of the dead that Americans pay for health care and defense combined.

Architecture evolved to meet the demand for increasingly refined theaters of the afterlife, in what might be the first recorded account of "keeping up with the Joneses." Three main types of tombs were built in Egypt: mastabas, pyramids, and rock-hewn crypts. The earliest royal tombs were mastabas, below-ground-level structures with wooden, and later stone, roofs covered with earth. In plan, these final resting places resembled a house, with several small rooms around a large central space containing the body and the funerary offerings.

For nearly four centuries the mastaba was the grave of choice and became more refined and complex with each passing dynasty. Elaborate clusters of these tombs were located at the ancient riverfront town of Saqqâra, where the first pyramid would appear later. Styles developed much more slowly back then, but by the twenty-eighth century B.C., Egyptians were hungry for a new architectural fashion to die for. (Ancient societies, like today's nouveau riche, found strange vehicles for their architectural endeavors. The Egyptians were a lot like Donald Trump and his cronies who built extravagant temples of commerce along Madison Avenue in the 1980s thinking that the good life would continue forever.)

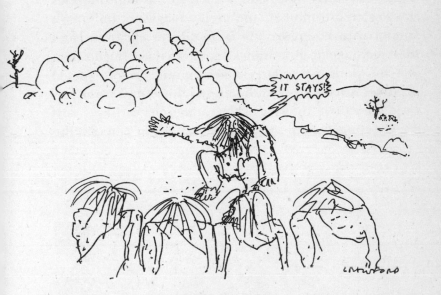

IT STAYS!

THE FIRST ANNUAL CONFERENCE ON ARCHITECTURAL PRESERVATION

THE FIRST ARCHITECT TO MAKE A NAME FOR HIMSELF—AND HE DIDN'T HAVE AN AGENT

The oldest documented pyramid was built as the burial place of King Zoser (2630 B.C.), not too far from the

Saqqâra mastabas. It's the first structure ever credited to an architect. The fellow who got the honors was Imhotep. You might say he was the Frank Lloyd Wright of the Nile. With an ego to match his talents, Imhotep branched out and was later deified for his contributions as a healer, astronomer, and even a magician. Imhotep's memorial to Zoser was the largest, most elaborate, and most technologically advanced tomb to date. In addition, it is the world's first large-scale monument constructed of stone. A handful of Imhotep's architectural plans survived, and these drawings show numerous revisions during the course of construction. How appropriate that the

The Step Pyramid of Saqqâra set a new standard in tomb design.

PAPYRUS: LESSON TO LEARN IN RECYCLING
. . . .
Plentiful in Egypt in antiquity, papyrus was a strong and pliable reed that grew like crabgrass along the Nile. These hardy stalks were carefully cut lengthwise into strips, then laid out flat and pressed to make paper. Five thousand years ago, papyrus was cheap, ubiquitous, and multifunctional. It was also used to craft sails, boats, and clothing, in addition to its more famous function as a writing material. But no more. Today that once bountiful, indigenous plant is nearly extinct.

first documented structure by an architect had no fewer than five changes of plans.

Imhotep's masterpiece for King Zoser, known as the Step Pyramid of Saqqâra, actually started out as a mastaba, but was expanded outward and upward. The architect utilized small blocks, about the size of today's traditional red bricks, rather than large stone masses. The building was supported with pillars, which were made to resemble bundles of papyrus reeds, carefully engaged to the walls. The edifice grew like a stacked square wedding cake, clad in white limestone. Imhotep surrounded his "stairway to heaven" with other stone buildings arranged to form an intricate courtyard. Like a grand processional to the afterlife, the original approach to the pyramid was through a tall gateway and continued along a corridor lined with slender limestone columns. Today, the walls of the court and some of the ancillary buildings have been reconstructed after lying in ruins for centuries.

A NEW AND IMPROVED PLACE IN THE SUN: THE 10,000-MAN JOB SITE

Zoser's Step Pyramid had stood almost a century when the first crypt in the shape of a true, straight-sided pyramid was built by King Seneferu in the desert at Dahshur. However, King Seneferu was soon outdone by none other than his son, King Cheops, at the riverfront city of Giza, which today is a suburb of Cairo.

Commanding thousands and thousands of skilled masons and craftsmen (some were volunteers and some less-willing participants), Cheops set out to build a tomb to surpass all others in quality and scale. He succeeded, and then he inspired his son and grandson-in-law to build their own monuments right next door. Built during the Fourth Dynasty, the Great Pyramid of Cheops and the subsequent designs for Chephren and Mykerinos form a dynamic trio. But Cheops kept a tight rein on

YOU SAY "KHUFU," I SAY "CHEOPS"

Like the song about "tomaytoes" and "tomahtoes," no one seems to agree on the spelling of the pharaoh who commissioned the Great Pyramid. Sir Banister Fletcher, the late British architectural historian who wrote the definitive book on the history of architecture (it's over 1,600 pages long, so don't tackle it unless you're really serious), calls him Cheops. Vincent Scully, who has taught the definitive history-of-architecture course at Yale University for more than forty-five years, calls him Khufu. Vincent Scully, the television sports announcer, couldn't be reached for comment.

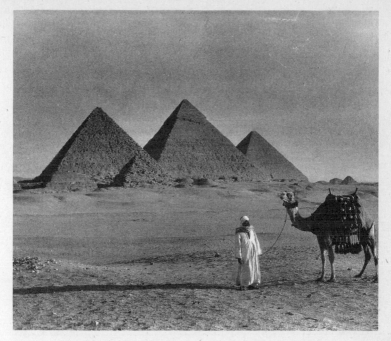

The Pyramids of Giza: Papa Bear (Cheops), Mama Bear (Chephren), and Baby Bear (Mykerinos).

his offspring—they didn't attempt to upstage dear old Dad, whose edifice is called the Great Pyramid of Cheops and is immortalized on every pack of Camel cigarettes.

The Cheops Pyramid measures 756 feet, is square in plan, and covers an area of about 13 acres. It soars 480 feet high and contains more than 2 million blocks of stone, each weighing over 2.5 tons. The four sides, each facing a compass point, are almost perfect equilateral triangles and meet the ground at roughly 51 degrees. The pyramids are striking displays of engineering, built by a society whose technology consisted of copper hand tools, the lever, and a lot of human muscle power. The fine Tura limestone for the casing was quarried across the Nile and ferried over by boat.

The original entrance of the Cheops Pyramid was located on the north face and set deliberately off center. The door was sealed at the time of burial and covered by casing stones. From this intentionally obscure "front door," a corridor descends through the core and into native rock. A hallway leads to the Queen's Chamber— a misnomer because no queen was buried there. Before this room was completed, it was sealed off as an elaborate ruse to foil grave robbers. From here the ascending corridor opens up to a splendid granite-lined passageway with a seven-sectioned, corbelled ceiling. (A corbelled ceiling has nothing to do with sparkling wine. It's a projecting carved or molded block of stone, which supports the beams of a roof or vault.) This leads to the King's Chamber, the final resting place, a tall and narrow room containing five compartments stacked one above the next. Grave robbers got to the booty thousands of years ago, so today nothing is left in the chamber but the granite sarcophagus, without its lid, that once held the pharaoh's body.

WHAT'S THAT CRAZY CAT DOING IN THE DESERT?

The second pyramid of the triad, and the best preserved of the bunch, was built for Chephren, son of Cheops. Centuries of wind and blowing sand have taken their toll on all the pyramids of Egypt, but Chephren's still boasts much of its original stone cladding. Near the apex, much of the limestone casing is intact, and fragments along the base indicate that lower courses were clad in granite. Next to the pyramid is his Valley Temple, which also is substantially intact. It's a serious statement in stone, with no delicate carvings of papyrus or flowers, only the ponderous solidity of unadorned granite facings. A deliberately dark and mysterious structure, the Valley Temple housed the ceremonies of purification, mummification, and other top-secret religious rituals.

THE ORIGINAL TOP-TEN LIST, MINUS THREE

Around 200 B.C., an out-of-work poet named Antipater drew up a list of seven magnificent structures and came up with the catchy title "The Seven Wonders of the World."

Antipater was not necessarily the first to catalog such a list, nor will David Letterman, with his nightly roster of contemporary wonders, be the last. There is some debate about a couple of Antipater's entries, but most scholars and third graders accept this version:

★ Great Pyramid of Egypt (2680 B.C.)
★ Hanging Gardens of Babylon (605–563 B.C.)
★ Statue of Zeus at Olympia (400 B.C.)
★ Temple of Artemis at Ephesus (300 B.C.)
★ Mausoleum of Halicarnassus (340–300 B.C.)
★ Colossus of Rhodes (304–292 B.C.)
★ Lighthouse of Alexandria (270 B.C.)

At no time in history did all seven stand simultaneously, and only the Cheops Pyramid survives today.

Chephren's four-sided edifice might be smaller than Dad's, but it's Junior's face that lives in history—in the form of a monstrous, enigmatic brute, the Great Sphinx. This narcissistic, artistic display was chiseled from a mass of stone left standing in an adjacent quarry. Looking eastward toward sunrise over the Nile, the Sphinx bears the head of Chephren (decked out in imperial headgear, false beard, and cobra brow ornament) on the body of a recumbent lion.

The "baby bear" of the pyramid trio belongs to Mykerinos, Chephren's son-in-law. It's significantly smaller, but an engineering feat of sophisticated proportions with elaborate tomb chambers.

WHERE HAVE ALL THE PYRAMIDS GONE?

Pharaohs who reigned after the three kings buried at Giza didn't attempt to build bigger pyramids, and the Giza Pyramids were never rivaled. No longer could god-rulers command the allocation of so much effort on a tomb, so they decided to throw in a few outbuildings, such as separate temples in honor of the ever-popular sun god, Re.

King Mentuhotep was an early doyen of changing funerary fashion. Although he made a name for himself by ending a civil war and reuniting the country around 2050 B.C., it was his tomb that ensured him a place in the architectural history books. Mentuhotep chose the impressive bay of Deir-el-Bahri, along the west bank of the Nile near the then-capital city of Thebes.

His burial compound is terraced on two main levels at the base of a steep natural cliff. The valley temple has long since disappeared, but the stepped terraces still

Building Your Architectural Vocabulary

Arch: A structure of wedge-shaped blocks over an opening that holds together when supported only from the sides.

Axis: An imaginary straight line about which parts of a building or groups of buildings are arranged.

Barrel vault: The simplest form of vaulting; a continuous semicircular vault that extends along a straight line.

Column: A freestanding upright supporting member with a circular shaft.

Hypostyle: A type of building that features a flat roof supported on massed rows of columns, giving a forest-like appearance.

Pillar: A detached upright supporting member with a square or polygonal section.

Pylon: Rectangular truncated tower flanking the gateway of an Egyptian temple.

exist. At the center of the outward-looking temple was a solid stone platform that supported a pyramid form. But this pyramid with a dummy burial chamber, or cenotaph, below was a ruse to mislead potential grave robbers. His actual crypt is what came to be known as a corridor tomb. His body is buried deep in the cliff, approached by a long underground tunnel that started in the small courtyard behind the temple.

TEMPLE, TEMPLE, WHO'S IN THE TEMPLE?

Five hundred years later, another ambitious ruler, Queen Hatshepsut, adopted this landscaped terrace style for her burial compound. Hatshepsut first came to power as regent for her young stepson, Thutmose, at the death of her husband. She soon seized the monarchy and ruled in her own right. She declared herself to be the daughter of the gods, and set out to ensure she had a proper royal burial.

She tapped architect Senmut to design her eternal resting spot and chose a site right next door to Mentuhotep, her stylistic precursor. Hatshepsut's extravaganza is a three-terraced affair, rising toward the base of the cliffs. Each terrace is ringed with a double colonnade.

This variety of mortuary temple was a hit with the hoi polloi, and soon more of these structures started to dot the landscape. Called cult temples, these sacred spots were devoted to the popular worship of the ancient and mysterious gods.

WHAT'S GOD GOT TO DO WITH IT?

The Temple of Amon at Karnak was the grandest of the cult variety. But it was slow in coming. For more than a thousand years (1530–323 B.C.), the shrines of this huge temple complex were constantly being expanded and restored. A massive stone wall surrounded the immense compound, which included a series of shrines, chapels, colonnades, elaborate courtyards, and a sacred lake. The main temple consisted of a series of pylons built at various times, with halls sandwiched between them. Beyond the second collection of pylons was the hypostyle hall, with 134 structural columns shaped in the form of papyrus plants. The central columns of the hall were sur-

*Central aisle of the hypostyle hall at Karnak—
Egypt's decorative answer to drywall construction.*

rounded by multiple rows of short, stout columns. At the
end of the sequence was the most holy sanctuary, where
the statue of the god lived.

An avenue of ram-headed sphinxes led from a dock
on the Nile to the first great pylon wall of the Amon
Temple complex. A second avenue lined with more
stone rams connected Karnak with the Temple at Luxor,
another "must-see." During the annual religious festival,
the statue of Amon at Karnak was carried through the
streets to visit his buddies at Luxor.

THE TIMES THEY ARE A-CHANGING. SLOWLY, THOUGH.

The Temple at Luxor, like its neighbor at Karnak, was
the product of hundreds of years of building. It was a
sequential arrangement with courtyards, impressive colonnades, lots of sphinxes, and a most-sacred sanctuary.
The hypostyle hall was never finished, leaving two impressive rows of high columns standing alone. Rameses
II, the powerful pharaoh who lived from 1304 to 1237
B.C. added a few ancillary buildings and statues of himself to the compound.

But when it came time to build his own final resting
place, Rameses II chose Abu Simbel. This temple-and-
tomb combo, with its four gigantic stone likenesses of
himself, is one of the most magnificent of the rock-hewn
mortuary complexes. The great house of worship shares
the hillside with a small temple, or Queen's Chapel, built
by Rameses for his wife, Nefertari. On its facade are four
standing figures of the king and two of the queen.

CRUISE THE NILE WITHOUT LEAVING HOME

On July 2, 1798, Napoleon landed in Egypt with thousands of soldiers intent on extending his empire into northern Africa. However, an accompanying group of historians probably did more lasting damage to Egypt than the military campaign. The historians took the Rosetta Stone—a carved basalt tablet inscribed by priests of the ruler Ptolemy V—back to Paris. A young French scholar named Champollion used the stone's side-by-side texts in Greek and in hieroglyphs to decipher the mystery of the Egyptian picture language.

Egypt soon became the antiquity of choice for Continentals, as well as Americans and Brits who wanted their own piece of the rock. Thanks to explorers, plunderers, and grave robbers, much of Egypt is on view around the world.

However, this involuntary export didn't begin with Napoleon; Roman emperors started the trend before the first century B.C. The obelisk in the Piazza of San Giovanni in Rome was removed hundreds of years earlier from the Temple of Amon. A monolith of red granite, it is the largest known obelisk.

Other ancient structures have found new homes more recently. Engineers in the 1960s working on the Aswan Dam weren't about to let a few antiquities stand in the way of progress. When the dammed Nile threatened to inundate the Temple of Dendur, the whole complex was dismantled and stored on an island in the middle of the river. Following a huge fund-raising drive in New York City, a new glazed wing of the Metropolitan Museum of Art was constructed to house the temple. It's a great exhibit, but it does seem a little out of place.

WONDER WHAT THE POOR PEOPLE WERE DOING?

Clay models left in tombs indicate that ordinary dwellings were constructed of crude brick with flat or arched roofs. Although little remains of the simple residences of the older cities of Thebes and Memphis, ruins of barrack-like worker housing exist near the pyramid sites at the cities of Giza and El Kahun, the home of the pyramid complex of Sesostris II (1897–1878 B.C.). The best preserved of these so-called "pyramid cities" is Deir-el-Medina, adjacent to the royal corridor tombs in the arid mountains on the west side of the Nile near Thebes. This commune endured for four centuries, housing the artists and craftsmen who worked on the crypts of the pharaohs. At Deir-el-Medina's peak, more than seventy houses were located within the walled compound with another fifty residences outside the wall. Workers usually toiled in the tombs for ten days at a time, and returned home at the end of their shift.

Their labors have proven to be worth the effort. For thousands of years civilization flourished along the Nile. Through all the regimes, their architecture remained stately, sober, single-minded, and most of all, stable. The very repetitiveness of their designs is what made them so memorable or created what is called the "the grand monotony" of the Egyptian landscape. Who are we to question the power of the pyramid?

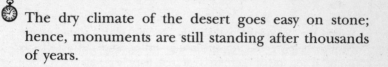

SUMMARY

⊘ The Egyptians left a wealth of information about their civilization through their architecture.

⊘ They built large structures that show a great understanding of engineering, esthetics, and design.

⊘ The dry climate of the desert goes easy on stone; hence, monuments are still standing after thousands of years.

⊘ Egypt delivered the world its first named architect—Imhotep.

⊘ The Egyptians were a religious people concerned with death and eternity—reflected in the time and effort lavished on tombs and temples.

⊘ The civilization gave the world the pyramid, an enduring architectural icon that still manages to look modern. (See I. M. Pei's recent addition to the Louvre, Chapter 9.)

CHAPTER 2

ANCIENT NEAR EAST
(5000 B.C.–400 B.C.)

YOU MUST REMEMBER THIS

Called the "cradle of civilization," the ancient societies of the Near East get credit for inventing writing and the art of city living. Their urban centers featured temples; palaces; a complex infrastructure of canals, bridges, roads, and fortifications; and a flashy civic icon, the ziggurat, a temple tower in the form of a stepped pyramid. Life on the Tigris and Euphrates rivers had its ups and downs, like any five-millennium civilization. Still, compared to the more recent Saddam Hussein, the Shah of Iran, and the Ayatollah, good old Hammurabi, Nebuchadnezzar, and Xerxes seem pretty sane.

MOST FAMOUS FOR

★ White Temple at Warka (3500–3000 B.C.)
★ Temple Oval at Khafaje (2650–2350 B.C.)
★ Ziggurat of Ur (2125 B.C.)
★ Citadel of Khorsabad and the Palace of Sargon II (722–705 B.C.)
★ Palace of Persepolis, built by Darius I and Xerxes I (518–465 B.C.)

DOWN BY THE RIVERSIDE

Civilization in the Near East flourished in the rich alluvial plain of the Tigris and Euphrates rivers under the name Mesopotamia, which means "in the middle of the rivers." Unlike desert-ringed Egypt, which was flourishing at about the same time, Mesopotamia lacked natural defensive boundaries and throughout its long history was usually in the middle of some kind of political fracas. Wars, revolutions, edicts, referendums, plagues, dynasties, as well as tragic love affairs, rebuffs and reunions were widespread throughout Sumeria, Assyria, Babylonia, and Persia. Not much has changed. Ancient Mesopotamia today encompasses parts of modern-day Syria, Turkey, Iran, and the not-so-peaceful Iraq, still overrun by other people's Patriot missiles and F-16 fighter planes.

The long history of the region is complex and tangled. The architectural account is not as well documented. In Mesopotamia, stone and timber suitable for building were not locally obtainable. The building materials of choice were sun-dried and kiln-fired clay bricks, which were significantly less permanent than stone. As a result, a majority of the ancient cities of Mesopotamia are today little more than great mounds of clay that sit in fierce heat against a flat desert landscape.

IN THE BEGINNING

The Sumerian people began setting up housekeeping in some of the world's first acknowledged cities around the thirty-sixth century B.C., in southern Mesopotamia. As the population of these nascent urban centers grew, they set up governing authorities. Separation of church and state was unheard of, so the ruler conveniently doubled as top priest. The Temple of Tepe Gawra was one of the earliest of these civic-and-religious compounds, with three temples set in a line.

The largest city in this early boom period was Warka, which had a walled perimeter of more than six miles. From written accounts, we know that almost one-third of the city was occupied by temples and other public buildings. Even the earliest real estate developers chose to

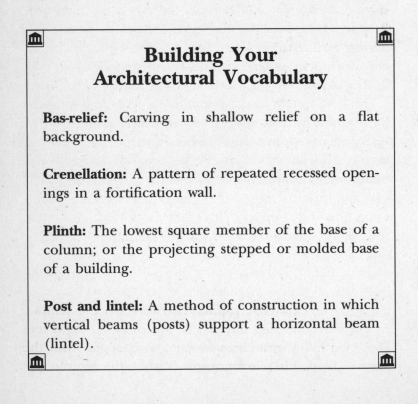

Building Your Architectural Vocabulary

Bas-relief: Carving in shallow relief on a flat background.

Crenellation: A pattern of repeated recessed openings in a fortification wall.

Plinth: The lowest square member of the base of a column; or the projecting stepped or molded base of a building.

Post and lintel: A method of construction in which vertical beams (posts) support a horizontal beam (lintel).

devote valuable downtown real estate to more glamorous functions than affordable housing.

Accordingly, there were several holy "must-sees" in beautiful downtown Warka. One of the most striking was the Pillar Hall, which stood on a brick terrace and included two rows of massive columns, decorated with a cone mosaic pattern suggestive of a palm trunk.

Not too far away, perched atop an artificial mountain, was Warka's White Temple. The base was irregularly shaped and rose 40 feet high. This temple is considered to be the precursor of Mesopotamia's famous ziggurats. The walls of this ziggurat ancestor were sloped and striped with diagonal fluting. The central hall was flanked on both sides by a series of smaller rooms. The temple had a doorway on each of the four elevations, and the main entrance was set off center along the longer side of the building. Rather than being set on a straight line, the various buildings of the compound were set in a skewed alignment giving the temple a "bent-axis" approach to the sanctuary. Shallow buttresses were the main source of ornamentation in the hall and along the external walls.

A SQUARE PEG IN AN OVAL WALL

At Khafaje, an ancient city northeast of modern Baghdad, the architects preferred a different geometry, not to mention innovative foundation work for the temple. The ground was dug out to a depth of about eight feet and then filled with clean white sand brought from the desert. Atop this pile of virgin silicon, the temple was safe from impurities. It was the kind of precaution you'd take today if you were building your house on a toxic waste dump. The whole compound was safely ensconced within two concentric oval walls and arranged in three ascending levels. The four-sided shrine itself was located on the highest terrace, and a great stairway ascending from the courtyard connected the stepped platforms. The artificial mound took on great meaning and a higher purpose. The temple was visible for miles across the flat landscape of Mesopotamia, and the added altitude allowed the people to feel they were a little closer to heaven.

Early City Slickers

Along the lower Euphrates River was the Sumerian walled city of Ur, the site of one of the best preserved of the Mesopotamian ziggurats. The monument at Ur was the handiwork of Ur-Nammu, who ruled the roost from 2124 to 2107 B.C. When Ur-Nammu came to power, there were the beginnings of a city, but like any good ruler, he devoted energy to public works. Nothing tarnishes a rising political star like potholes or a second-rate ziggurat.

Archaeological excavations of Ur reveal a twisted network of streets, one of the first examples of a shopping bazaar, and a manufacturing complex housing iron-works, tanneries, and looms. The city had its own social hierarchy. The wealthier classes lived in spacious houses with a dozen or more rooms, arranged on two stories, whitewashed inside and out. Domestic servants generally lived on the ground floor, while the family resided on the upper level.

At the Royal Cemetery in Ur, Sumerian builders were experimenting with all kinds of new rooflines for royal tombs. Like hemlines, roofs are a quick study in architectural fashion. Around 2100 B.C. you had your choice of a true arch, a true barrel vault, or the ever-popular, but more sophisticated, dome.

BABYLON: MOTHER OF HARLOTS

Babylon, situated along the Euphrates, was one of the most famous Mesopotamian cities. It was voluptuous, opulent, decadent, a hot spot on the caravan route, and

YOU THINK YOUR MALPRACTICE PREMIUMS ARE HIGH?

Contemporary architects complain about liability insurance and argue that lawyers are too quick to sue. The Code of Hammurabi, that most famous set of laws carved onto a stele of black stone, addressed legal and moral concerns of the day. But it also spelled out some pretty specific regulations on such issues as trade, commerce, and taxes, and it called for tough penalties for faulty and flimsy workmanship in building. Back in the good old days before malpractice premiums, if an architect built a house that collapsed and killed the client, the architect could be put to death. If a slave of the client was killed as a result of construction failures, the architect had to replace the servant.

was characterized by strident civic propaganda and conspicuous consumption. Babylon first blossomed during the rule of Hammurabi. From 1792 to 1750 B.C., Babylon was the capital city of his powerful empire. Throughout its history, the city was regularly invaded and often fell to foreign armies. It was rebuilt on numerous occasions, with each remodeling providing bigger fortifications, taller citadels, more elaborate palaces, better all-round

TOWER OF BABEL: STAIRWAY TO HEAVEN OR SCAFFOLDING TO HELL?

Babylon's most celebrated ziggurat, immortalized in the Bible as the Tower of Babel, sat on a 295-foot square base with a triple stairway approach. Seven stepped platforms formed an ascending spiral. The summit temple, which peaked at almost three hundred feet, was faced with blue glazed bricks and inlaid gold.

Even back then, it was hard to know if rulers were building magnificent edifices to honor God or to honor themselves. But to the people of Mesopotamia who built the ziggurat, the massive stepped monument was intended to be a ladder of humble reverence. It was to remain a benevolent tower reaching up toward divinity.

To the Jewish people, who arrived in Babylon as prisoners with their own commandments about "graven images," this "Mountain of Heaven" was sacrilegious. With a different philosophical temperament than the builders of the ziggurat, the Jews believed that the tower was evil and would be destroyed. They must have had an "in" at the planning board; nothing remains today but the legend.

decorations, and more styles for architectural historians to puzzle over.

Babylon's glory days were under the reign of Nebuchadnezzar (605–563 B.C.). He lavishly reconstructed the city after an Assyrian assault about a hundred years earlier had pretty much leveled the place. Nebuchadnezzar surrounded the city with an imposing wall and built a chain of temples, grand avenues, bridges, and a luxuri-

The legendary Tower of Babel was thought to be a quick ascent to heaven. A painting by Pieter Brueghel in 1563 shows the fascination didn't wane.

ous palace along the river. For getting around town, he constructed great processionals, including the formal approach to the palace along the Avenue of Lions and through the Ishtar Gate. This grand boulevard, 73 feet wide, was built of brick covered with a primitive version of asphalt and topped with huge slabs of limestone. The concourse was lined with thick mud-brick walls covered with thousands of colorful glazed tiles and detailed with reliefs of fierce animals called *sirrushes*. These images were more than mere decoration; their function was to frighten away evil spirits.

HITCH YOUR GARDEN
TO A ZIGGURAT

Last, but certainly not least, was Nebuchadnezzar's Hanging Gardens of Babylon. Legend has it (and archeological digs indicate) that the king built the elaborate gardens to cheer up his homesick wife, Queen Amyitis, who was born in a green and mountainous region of Persia. Babylon's celebrated garden was reported to have measured 900 by 600 feet in plan and to have risen to the height of a 30-story skyscraper. Covered terraces stacked one above another were supported by cube-shaped pillars. A sophisticated system of pumps and pipes continuously lifted water from the Euphrates River to support the elaborate plantings, including large trees, lush vines, and colorful flowers. (Maybe princes Charles and Andrew should have concentrated more on the landscaping at Buckingham Palace when *their* princesses started getting restless.)

UP RIVER WITH AN ATTITUDE

The Assyrian Empire was centered north of Babylon, covering the territory of modern-day Iraq. While other Mesopotamian contemporary cultures lavished great effort on building temples to keep the gods happy, the Assyrian rulers focused on their own worldly comforts by building elaborate palaces. In the walled city of Khorsabad, King Sargon II (722–705 B.C.) built an extravaganza that was never rivaled. Covering nearly 23 acres, the Palace of Sargon was a complex maze of large and small

DON'T TOUCH THAT APPLE

Mesopotamia is considered by some archeologists, Sunday school teachers, and Hebrew scholars to be the Garden of Eden of Biblical fame. The land was fertile, there was a long growing season, and fruit trees bore abundant harvests. It seems like as good a place as any to commit the original sin.

Other hot spots in the region get prominent play in the Good Book. In Jeremiah, it is written that "the broad walls of Babylon shall be utterly broken, and her high gates shall be burned with fire; and the people shall labor in vain, and the folk in the fire, and they shall be weary." Sounds a little like contemporary L.A.

And in the final pages of the New Testament, the Book of Revelation describes Babylon with some pretty strong words: "Alas, alas, that great city, that was clothed in fine linen, and purple, and scarlet, and decked with gold, and precious stones, and pearls. For in one hour so great riches is come to nought."

courts, corridors, and rooms. The king and his extended family (i.e., lots of wives) lived in majestic digs within the compound. The monarch's administrative functions and sacred duties were housed nearby in their own elaborate buildings.

The royal compound was set atop terraces the height of the city's wall. The approach to the palace from the city was through a massive citadel gate and across an open square. A broad ramp provided a formal approach to a grand courtyard, which was flanked by huge, ornate towers and guarded by man-headed winged bulls. The inner sanctum was a long narrow Throne Room, anchored at the end with an appropriately ostentatious throne. There was a ziggurat, a seven-tiered structure with a winding ramp and paneled with colorful glazed tiles, but the temple tower was modest in relationship to the royal residence.

Sargon's son Sennacherib moved the capital to Nineveh. The city thrived for several generations and boasted mighty walls, a citadel, and a more than ample palace. Unlike its downstream neighbors, Nineveh was set on a high table of limestone, hard rock, and alabaster. Unfortunately, the natives were slow to take full advantage of these natural resources, choosing instead to continue to use sun-dried and kiln-baked bricks. So Nineveh simply went to pieces with time, leaving scant built reminders of a great civilization. Where a grand city once stood, nothing remains but a vague hill.

PERSIA: MORE THAN JUST RUGS

Cyrus the Great, founder of the first Persian Empire in the mid-sixth century B.C., made his headquarters in the city of Pasargadae. By the time his successor Darius I (522–486 B.C.) ascended the throne, the power center had moved 30 miles south to a new ceremonial capital at Persepolis. Built on a 40-foot-tall platform, measuring 1500 by 1000 feet in plan, the palace was faced in well-laid local stone bound with iron clamps. The approach along the northwest elevation was a magnificent flight of steps, wide and shallow enough for horses to ascend. A secondary entrance along the south side of the complex opened onto the "Apadana," a grand audience hall enlivened with thirty-six stone columns within its 20-foot-thick walls. Beyond this wall was Darius's personal palace and the administrative buildings he constructed.

Under the reign of Xerxes I (486–465 B.C.), the pal-

Remains of the stairway of the Tripylon at Persepolis show the wealth of architectural motifs that adorned this ancient city.

ace compound was expanded and embellished. Xerxes chose to build close by, and constructed his palace at the southwest corner of the royal compound. His most glorious addition was the Hall of the Hundred Columns. This was his' throne room—and what a room it was! One hundred 37-foot-tall columns supported a flat cedar roof. Although the use of more stone provide bits and pieces of permanence in sculptures and artifacts, the ruins of this great city give an inaccurate impression of its one-time grandeur.

In spite of the fact that few architectural monuments survive intact, the complex Mesopotamian region had its share of good design. Even more important than the icon, the ziggurat, the peoples of the Tigris and Euphrates rivers gave the world its first taste of city living and

The Hall of the Hundred Columns was one example of the society's structural excesses.

the fundamentals of good urban planning. Too bad those responsible for contemporary American suburbia didn't look back five thousand years for a few good models.

SUMMARY

The peoples of Mesopotamia made the first conscious attempt to live in cities. Their urban centers were architecturally sophisticated and efficient models of civic government.

In a land without stone or wood, the material of choice was sun-dried brick, which didn't hold up in the harsh climate. Few of their monuments have survived.

Mesopotamians were interested in more than mere function: they decorated their buildings with complex systems of vertical pilasters and ornate brickwork and decorated surfaces with brilliant glazed ornaments and bas-relief images.

Collectively these peoples were a bit paranoid, but not without reason. Their palaces and temples were usually surrounded by elaborate fortress walls that rarely stopped invading neighbors.

CHAPTER 3

ANCIENT GREECE
(1900 B.C.–100 B.C.)

YOU MUST REMEMBER THIS

Sensitive intellectuals of antiquity, the Greeks developed the prescription for Classical architecture. They started with simple post-and-lintel construction and went on to perfect these forms to develop architecture's original "kit of parts"—the Doric, Ionic, and Corinthian orders—undoubtedly the most widely used decorative elements of Western architecture. Like no one before them, the Greeks mastered the sacred rules governing the harmony of form to build perfectly proportioned buildings.

MOST FAMOUS FOR

★ Palace of King Minos, Knossos, Crete (1900–1400 B.C.)
★ The Acropolis (500–300 B.C.), the hilltop cluster of famous Greek structures:
  The Parthenon (447–436 B.C.)
  The Propylaea (436–431 B.C.)
  Temple of Athena Nike (427 B.C.)
  Erechtheion (421–405 B.C.)
★ Theater of Epidaurus (350 B.C.)

EARLY HISTORY

The first great civilization of the Aegean world were the Minoans, who flourished on the island of Crete and reached their height of power between 3000 and 1450 B.C. The island's economy thrived and its kings built some pretty impressive structures, including the Palace of Minos in Knossos. A British archaeologist, Arthur Evans, discovered the ancient city of Knossos in the early part of the twentieth century. The city was organized on a modular plan set on the side of a hill facing the sea. In an exceptional excavation, Evans and his group unearthed a complete town with a grand palace, marketplace, theaters, and housing. Minoan architecture wasn't nearly as elegant or sophisticated as that of the later Greeks, but Minoan homes did have one remarkable luxury: bathrooms with running water and flush toilets.

The island of Crete, with its large and complex palaces, laid a foundation for a future culture in Athens that would provide the most important architectural developments of all time.

On the mainland, a second society, the Mycenaeans, coincided in time with the Minoans and eventually superseded them. The Mycenaean culture was militaristic to the bone. Their houses were protected by sophisticated fortifications. The Palace of Tiryns is a hilltop citadel, surrounded by massive defensive walls (showing their designers' significantly more bellicose personality). The most famous feature of the fortress is the Lion Gate.

The Mycenaean's famous Treasury of Atreus, also known as the Tomb of Agamemnon, is one of the premium burial spots of the Greek Isles. Called a *tholos,* or beehive tomb, it features thirty-four rings of masonry, capped with a stone-dome vault buried below an earthen mound. But Mycenaean civilization faded around 1100 B.C., propelling Greece into its own mini-Dark Ages, before Athens blossomed around the seventh century B.C.

ONE HELLUVA HELLENISTIC PERIOD

Religion played a major role in Greek life. The Greeks believed they could buy the favor of their gods with gold, silver, and animal sacrifice. So it's not surprising that

The Grand Staircase of the Palace of Minos featured inverted columns that look like upturned tree trunks.

the temples of ancient Greece were the most important structures of the day.

The earliest Greek temples resembled the Mycenaean *megaron,* or house of the chief. It was a simple rectangular hall with a pitched roof and a front porch. The Greeks obviously liked the image because for most of their early temples they continued to use basically the same form. However, they didn't rest on their laurels, but tried relentlessly to perfect the simple structure, leading to continual changes in materials, proportion, and detailing. The oldest stone temple of which anything

THE FIRST THREE ORDERS OF BUSINESS

An order in architecture means a column with a base, shaft, and capital.

 The Doric is the original order and the foundation for the later refinements. Doric is the "plain Jane" of the trio, characterized by robust columns with sharp-edged flutings and no base.

The Ionic order is thought to have originated in Asia Minor, but it was perfected in Athens. Svelte and suave, it has as its distinctive feature the spiral scroll, or volute, which looks a bit like the curl of a ram's horn or the twirl of a chambered nautilus at the top of the capital.

Last but certainly not least is the Corinthian order—that's the fancy one. Its capital is an elaborate bouquet of acanthus leaves. Although the Corinthian order made its first appearance in Greek architecture in the fifth century, it took the Romans to embrace the excessive style and bring it to maturity.

substantial survives is the Temple of Hera at Olympia, a long, low, unpretentious Doric temple constructed at the end of the seventh century B.C.

ON A HILL FAR AWAY

Athens was supreme of all the Greek city-states. A city-state is a political structure where each town is a separate entity—sorta like the situation in the former Yugoslavia today. But Athens was a military power as well as the center of scholarship and the arts. Its patron, Athena, was goddess of wisdom and warfare—the perfect symbol for the town's schizoid personality. In 480 B.C., the Persians invaded Athens and pretty much destroyed it. However, the city rebounded, and a huge rebuilding program was launched by Pericles, a charismatic general and statesman who was elected *strategos* (that's like our commander-in-chief) every year from 443 to 429 B.C.

Pericles turned to his friend Phidias, master sculptor and designer, for ideas for a new and improved Athenian Acropolis, a cluster of buildings set on a dramatic limestone outcropping above the city proper that suffered in past battles. In less than forty-five years they had constructed what is without question one of the most famous groupings of buildings anywhere in the world.

Every great compound needs a great portal and the Acropolis is no exception. The monumental Propylaea (436–431 B.C.), or ceremonial gateway, framed the only point of access on the steep slopes of the Acropolis. Architect Mnesicles used the Doric order for the exterior and the Ionic inside and bridged two levels of the site to achieve a unique fusion of grandeur and modesty. It was the perfect introduction to the wonders that lay ahead.

The small but exquisite Temple of Athena Nike (427 B.C.), perched to the right of the Propylaea, is one of the oldest surviving Ionic buildings in Athens. Only

Building Your Architectural Vocabulary

Cella: The main section of a Classical temple.

Entablature: The big horizontal section that runs along the top of the columns. It consists of the architrave (the lower beam), frieze (the middle section, usually carved with intense ornamentation), and cornice (the projecting uppermost part).

Pediment: The big triangle that sits atop the entablature. It can be decorated or plain.

Podium: The continuous base on which a temple or other structure is built.

Portico: Colonnaded entry or porch of a building.

Rotunda: A building or room that is circular in plan.

Stoa: A detached colonnade.

about 18½ feet wide and 27 feet long, it has front and rear porticoes, each with four Ionic columns and a sculptured frieze around the top, but no pediment. Credit for this petite jewel goes to architect Callicrates. The Turks tore it down, but politely left the pieces strewn on the ground, so that it was possible to re-erect the precious little structure in 1835.

The best known of the Ionic temples, however, is the Erechtheion (421–405 B.C.). The plan is unusual. It has an irregular form and stands on different levels connected by steps. Externally, the temple has been restored, but nothing remains of the interior. Its trademark is a funky little porch perched along the

Temple of Athena Nike. I can't believe they built a temple to the sneaker 2,000 years before Michael Jordan even thought about playing basketball.

south side of the building. Instead of the usual columns, six draped maidens, or Caryatids, carved of marble hold up a flat marble roof.

Five of the Erechtheion girls are original. (The second from the left is a terra-cotta copy. The real McCoy is in the British Museum.)

NOTHING TO FEAR
. . . .
The Greek agora, or market, was the social and political hub of the city, serving as a meeting place and shopping mall. In Athens, the agora was originally an open space. It was gradually filled with buildings, including a great two-storied stoa, or colonnaded portico, that housed shops and offices and defined the east boundary. An assembly hall, town hall, gymnasium, and theater soon

---

(*continued*) . . . .

added to the downtown congestion. There was always
a frenzy of activity at the old agora. It was probably a
bit overwhelming and the high-stress environment could
have scared away a lot of shy Greeks. Nothing remains
of the original buildings, but the name caught on. Agora
is still the name for a groovy shopping area. But the
term took on larger implications. Agoraphobia is the
label given to the fear of leaving your house.

TOP DOG

Dominating the Acropolis is the Parthenon. A collaboration of three talented Athenians—the architects Ictinus
and Callicrates, and the sculpter Phidias—designed the
masterpiece. The Parthenon is the most perfect Doric
temple ever built and the ultimate accomplishment of
Classical Greece. It was one of the first really large marble buildings—erected before that precious stone was reserved for sculpture. The basic design of the temple is
simplicity itself—eight columns wide by seventeen long,
following the rule that the sides should have double the
number of the ends, plus one. The triangular pediments
at either end framed sculptures; along the top was an
awesome frieze representing men, maidens, and animals.

ALL THE WORLD'S A STAGE

In addition to their impeccable temples, the Greeks built
some great theaters. The most primitive performance

Today the Parthenon's roof might leak, but it's no fault of the architects. In 1687, during combat between the Turks and Venetians, it suffered massive damage in a shelling.

WHY THE PARTHENON LOOKS SO PERFECT

In many art forms, perfection sometimes requires ever-so-slight bending of the rules. For music to sound pure, intervals are delicately manipulated to sound harmonious. The Greeks developed sophisticated and very subtle optical corrections, called entases, to make a building look perfectly proportioned in spite of two-dimensional tricks played by the human eye.

They first refined the columns. When viewed against the sky, a column with perfectly straight edges would appear thinner in the middle so the Greeks curved the upper part of the shaft slightly outward. This minor dis-

(continued)

tortion compensates for the illusion and prevents the taper from leading the eye upward too quickly. For the platform base, or the stylobate, they used a slight convex curve—the highest point of the base is at the center and then it slopes down to the edges. All the columns lean inward, while the four corner columns are placed a tiny bit closer to their immediate neighbors. In reality, few components of the best Greek temples are actually horizontal or perpendicular.

The Theater at Epidaurus: A great place to catch a current blockbuster like Prometheus Bound, Oedipus Rex, *or* Electra.

spaces were little more than a hollow dug out on a hill-side. Here spectators could overlook a flat natural stage for ceremonies honoring Dionysus, that hedonist, hell-raising god of sex, drugs, and rock and roll—or something like that. (Legend has it that he was a smoker, too.) These raucous celebrations in honor of Dionysus spawned Greek drama and some pretty spectacular structures.

The Theater at Epidaurus (350 B.C.), designed by local architect Polycleitos, was the most perfect development of the theatrical form. It's an achievement that this great semicircular auditorium held 14,000 spectators, but it's the geometrical exactitude that really makes this place special. The architect played with proportions to create the optimal sight lines and acoustics. (It's a lesson that is often lost on the contemporary designers of those pitiful playhouses that profess to be multiplex movie theaters.)

SPORTS AS RELIGION

The Greeks were as fanatical about sports as contemporary Americans. They believed in bodybuilding as training for warfare and as a way of honoring the gods. There were local sporting competitions, but once every four years men from throughout the Greek world descended on Olympia for the Big Games. Success in the Olympics brought honor to the athlete's family and to his home-town, and big winners acquired almost mythical status not unlike today's celebrities. Temples and all kinds of facilities for the participants and spectators have been excavated on Olympia.

OTHER SACRED SPORTS

The impetus for the premium Greek temples came from the cities, but other important religious sanctuaries, including those at Delphi, Olympia, and Delos, grew up outside the urban areas.

Thought to be the center of the world, Delphi, located on the steep slopes of Mount Parnassus, was the home of the main shrine of the god Apollo. (He's the one who *didn't* like to have fun. He was way too busy being the god of law, reason, art, medicine, music, poetry, and everything else that was rational and morally upstanding.) The layout of the sanctuary around the Sacred Way, which zigzags up from the south, appears haphazard but is in fact brilliantly arranged to create a succession of breathtaking views. The Stadium at Delphi is located in the highest part of the ancient city. The stone starting grooves on the running track and many of the spectator seats that were cut into the mountainside still survive.

In all the arts and sciences, the ancient Greeks made incredible contributions. They laid the foundation for pretty much all of what would come to be known as Western Civilization. They set standards for intellectual processes and esthetic judgments. The Greeks excelled in almost every area, but their architecture is unquestionably one of the grandest achievements.

SUMMARY

🕰 The Greeks lived and built by the motto "quality, not quantity."

🕰 Buildings were works of art more than structural innovations, and as a result they remained subordinated to the landscape.

🕰 The Greeks invented Classical architecture. With their Doric, Ionic, and Corinthian orders, they refined their style and then passed it down through generations.

🕰 Though the Greeks gave the world its first taste of what was to be "civic" architecture, most of their great buildings were temples. They actually constructed relatively few secular structures.

🕰 The Greeks' architecture was rarely bold or dramatic; it was a blend of logic and sensitivity that created a harmonious tranquility that is without parallel.

🕰 Their theories of proportion and balance are a continuing influence today.

CHAPTER 4

ANCIENT ROME
(300 B.C.–A.D. 476)

YOU MUST REMEMBER THIS

It wasn't built in a day, and its buildings have lasted thousands of years. The Greeks were the sensitive intellectuals and the true artists who devised the formulas that produced the original Classical architecture. But the Romans were the pragmatics, who knew a good thing when they saw it. The Greeks built some exquisite temples on a hill; the Romans copied this popular style and combined it with sophisticated engineering to build great cities and enormous public works projects, as well as a few of their own impressive monuments to the gods.

MOST FAMOUS FOR

★ Pantheon, Rome, (25 B.C.–A.D. 124), not to be confused with the Parthenon
★ Pont du Gard, Nimes, France (A.D. 14)
★ Colosseum (A.D. 70–82)
★ Baths of Caracalla (A.D. 211–217)
★ Hagia Sophia, Constantinople (A.D. 532–537)

DUBIOUS BEGINNINGS

Legend has it that Rome was founded in 753 B.C. along the River Tiber by a mythical dude named Romulus. Set atop seven famous hills, Rome was ruled first by the Etruscans but within a few hundred years had come into its own. The Romans vanquished their neighbors one by one and extended their boundaries through war and military conquests. By the third century B.C., Rome led an impressive confederacy of Latin states, and within another three hundred years it would rule pretty much all of the Western world.

THE ROOTS OF ROMAN DESIGN

Rome's earliest building retained an Etruscan character. But by 250 B.C. the city was booming and needed a style befitting a growing empire. The founding fathers of "The Eternal City" were inspired by the grandeur of Greek architecture. Roman builders adopted the Classical idiom not just out of appreciation for the esthetic, but also because they knew it would play well in the Empire. In the hands of the Romans, Classicism became conspicuously civic in function and served as proclamations of Roman dominance throughout the land. The Greeks might have invented the Classical forms, but the Romans added a new level of engineering sophistication and then packaged and marketed the style as their own.

MORE THAN A PRETTY FACADE

The Greeks had relied almost exclusively on a basic post-and-lintel system of construction, but the Romans added a perfected method of arch-and-vault construction. Although the Romans didn't invent the arch, they exploited it with unprecedented expertise. They also discovered how to make concrete from stone rubble mixed with lime and a volcanic sand called pozzolana. This new material made it easier to build arches, barrel vaults, and domes, thus creating vast interior spaces less dependent on columns between the walls.

Whereas the Greeks had been subservient to their environment, the Romans' engineering know-how and innovative use of materials enabled them to impose order on nature and shape the landscape. New towns and colonial outposts were laid out according to rectangular grid plans, with buildings arranged in a logical hierarchy based on their relative importance. The Romans understood the importance of open public plazas and devoted as much attention to the space between buildings as to their walls and domes. As a result, today Italian cities still boast some of the greatest "outdoor rooms" of the world.

A FUNNY THING HAPPENED ON THE WAY TO THE FORUM

The forum in ancient Rome, like the Greek agora or today's suburban shopping mall, was the social hub of the city, serving as meeting place and market. The first

Roman forum, the Forum Romanum, developed in a valley swamp that had been drained by the Etruscans. Political facilities, including the senate houses and orators' platform, were located to the west, while religious structures were clustered to the east.

By the time of Julius Caesar, the old forum was so overcrowded that in 54 B.C. he built a new, larger forum, consisting of a large plaza enclosed on four sides by a portico accommodating shops. Located adjacent to the original, this new symmetrical forum was more elaborate than its predecessor and proved popular with the people. When Augustus became emperor, he too built a forum in his own honor. Subsequent emperors—Tiberius, Vespasian, and Nerva—followed suit. Finally Trajan (A.D. 98–113) completed the compound with a forum that contained a basilica, temple, market, and two libraries— one Greek and one Latin.

SOME LIKE IT HOT

The most revered shrine in the Imperial City was the Temple of Vesta, where the Vestal Virgins tended the sacred fire that signified the home hearth as the center and source of life and power. Located in the original Forum Romanum, the temple was founded as far back as the seventh century B.C., but was frequently destroyed by fire. (Maybe the Virgins were entertaining gentlemen callers rather than watching the holy flames, and things got a little too hot.) The temple was repeatedly rebuilt, most recently in A.D. 205 Only fragments survive, but we know that it featured a circular cella (that's the main section of the temple) surrounded by eighteen Corinthian columns.

Each ruler tried to outdo the last and leave his mark with grand commemorative statues and arches. In its final days, the Roman Forum was a dazzling collection of diverse buildings and splendid monuments, probably the most impressive grouping ever assembled in the Ancient World. It grew over the centuries without a cohesive organization, but its hodgepodge of styles, scales, and building types combined to create an effect with immense vitality and monumentality. In many civilizations, the rise of architectural excesses was a kind of overcompensation for the fall of political vitality. And so it went in Rome.

DON'T JUDGE A BUILDING BY ITS COVER

The Romans had a penchant for excess, in terms of architecture as well as their parties and personal relations. The esthetic functionalism of the Greeks gave way to a largely decorative treatment of the Classical orders. Columns were often placed along walls that were structurally sound without them. The entablatures of the Theater of Marcellus (23–13 B.C.), which appears to be supported by half columns, is actually carried by arches. The mundane structural functions of piers, buttresses, and pinnacles were usually disguised behind Classical ornament. In this their designers were not unlike the more recent group of architects called Postmodernist (see Chapter 13).

However, there is nothing excessive about the Pantheon, the ultimate monument and the best-preserved building of ancient Rome. Massive and imposing as it is, the Pantheon is a perfectly proportioned structure without an ounce of fat. The exterior of the Pantheon is relatively undistinguished. From most angles, it appears to be a solid cylindrical drum of reinforced concrete crowned with a simple, saucer-shaped dome. The front elevation presents a fine but not extraordinary portico with eight Corinthian columns supporting a low entablature and a fairly ordinary pediment.

But wait until you step inside. Definitely a WOW space! The interior dome turns out to be a perfect hemisphere. It rises from the top of the second tier of a three-tiered wall of faced concrete; support is lent by arches hidden within the walls. The ceiling features an elaborate configuration of coffers, or sunken panels. These niches are

The Pantheon's exterior is relatively straightforward.
It's that great rotunda that everybody copied.

foreshortened to exaggerate the perspective of the ceiling. However, the design is more than just esthetic: it reduces the weight of the dome. Then there's the ethereal lighting. This great space has no windows, only a single round hole, or oculus, 27 feet in diameter, at the top of the dome.

The Pantheon was originally built around 25 B.C. and dedicated to the seven planetary deities. Some long-dead architect is kicking himself for not hiring an agent, because no one knows who designed the masterpiece. The

THE ORIGINAL SPIN DOCTOR
OF ARCHITECTURE
. . . .
His full name is Marcus Vitruvius Pollio, but call him Vitruvius; everybody else does. Little is known of the life of Vitruvius, except what tidbits can be culled from his famous treatise, *On Architecture.* We do know he lived in Rome sometime in the first century B.C.

His famous handbook for Roman architects is divided into ten books. They cover almost every aspect of design, but he believed the Greek model was the best. Although Vitruvius lived nearly four hundred years after the glory days of Greek architecture, he documented the Greek style and manner of building. Research was tougher back then, so when he couldn't confirm facts he just made up explanations. Vitruvius did express a hope that his name would be honored in posterity. His pedantic theories are somewhat suspect, but he achieved recognition as the sole authority on ancient Classical architecture. When his writings were rediscovered during the Renaissance (see Chapter 9), his place in history was set.

building was almost completely destroyed by fire and was rebuilt in A.D. 120 by the powerful and popular Emperor Hadrian. The dome as we know it probably dates from the third century.

THE GRUESOMEST SHOW ON EARTH

The Romans were great spectators, so as it grew, the Empire built amphitheaters, circuses, and theaters for its citizens. The most famous of these is the Roman Colosseum, or Flavian Amphitheater (A.D. 70–80). Any building that featured death-dealing combat of gladiators and confrontations between hungry lions and martyrs demanded a spectacular enclosure. But even if the colosseum had hosted only lighthearted musical comedies, it would still deserve a place in architectural history.

The building is an ellipse 620 feet long. Four tiers of seats for more than 50,000 spectators were supported by a rigid honeycomb structure of vaults and arches—all disguised behind an elegant curved facade. The corridors, or arcades, between the piers formed an effective pedestrian circulation system, with access to the tiered seating via tunnels and steps. Two noteworthy concepts are attributed to the Colosseum: the separation of structure and applied decoration, and the use of all three Greek orders (Doric, Ionic, and Corinthian) stacked one above the other.

Even in ruins the Colosseum is an awesome monument, and it's easy to see why it was a model for amphitheaters throughout history. The building also is responsible for the word *arena,* which is the Latin word

*At the Colosseum every seat in the house
had an unobstructed view.*

for "sand." It was so called because of the sand that was
strewn on the ground to absorb the blood of the
combatants.

The great chariot races, immortalized by Charlton
Heston in the movie *Ben Hur*, got top billing at the circus. Famous charioteers were the idols of the day. They
regularly risked life and limb for less pay than your aver-
age third baseman, and they never once went on strike.
Nothing remains of the Circus Maximus, the oldest and
largest of the ancient racetracks. A few vestiges can still
be found in Rome of the Circus of Maxentius (A.D. 311).

DOMESTIC LIFE

Roman residential designs, of which much survive, were incredibly diverse to meet the needs of the variety of social classes. The biggest and best were the imperial palaces. Next in the design hierarchy were the country villas and the urbane city townhouses. And of course, there was worker housing, but not much of that remains.

Much does remain of Hadrian's Villa at Tivoli, built as a country retreat in a grand landscape. The city of Rome had grown, so the villa is now set pretty close to the heart of downtown. Walking around the grounds today, it is possible to imagine the one-time glory of this compound, which occupies a park nearly 10 miles square. During its heyday, there were ceremonial halls, apartment buildings, theaters, baths, colonnaded court-yards, and formal garden after formal garden.

NO ROOM FOR THE DEAD

Roman law prohibited burial within the city limits, so tombs were located along the main roads outside of town. One noteworthy monument to a dead person is the Mausoleum of Hadrian (A.D. 135–39). It's now located in Rome; the city borders must have grown in the past 1,900 years. His mausoleum became the Papa Castle of St. Angelo in the Middle Ages and it underwent major renovations.

WATER, WATER EVERYWHERE

Back before the days of Evian and Perrier, the Romans had to rely on their own devices to get lots of water to thirsty subjects, not to mention their elaborate fountains and public baths. The Romans figured out the simple hydrostatic law that water rises to its own level in closed pipes. Eleven great aqueducts poured daily more than 350 million gallons of water into Rome. Circuitous routes were often necessary, and great tiers of stone or concrete arches rose more than a hundred feet over ravines and low-lying places to give sufficient "head" to the water supply.

They were built to last and they did. Ruined aqueducts from Rome to Segovia, Spain, still stand as a reminder of the importance attached by the Romans to an adequate water supply. The well-preserved Pont du Gard (around A.D. 10) formed part of a magnificent system that extended more than 25 miles to bring water to the

The Pont du Gard outside Nimes, France,
was erected almost entirely without mortar.

Roman town of Nimes, France. Three tiers of arches rise more than 155 feet above the river Gard. Numerous aqueducts were constructed from the late fourth century B.C. onward, but none surpassed Pont du Gard in terms of engineering or esthetics.

RUB-A-DUB-DUB, DON'T WEAR YOUR TOGA IN THE TUB

The *thermae,* or palatial public baths, portray, even in their present-day ruined state, the mores of the pleasure-seeking people of Imperial Rome. Designed for luxurious bathing, the *thermae* became a social club for news, gossip, sports, socializing, and business, as well as the hippest of Rome's many pageants, the Bacchanalian orgy.

The palatial Baths of Caracalla (A.D. 211–217), now a mere skeleton of a building, was the epitome of the *thermae* philosophy. The immense vaulted hall had symmetrical wings along either side. Decoration was an integral part of the building—there were marble colonnades and opulent statuary. Floors were paved with glazed mosaics and marble, walls were stuccoed and painted with sumptuous murals, and grand sculptures lined the great hall.

The Baths of Diocletian (A.D. 302–306) was similar to Caracalla, but even larger, accommodating more than 3,000 bathers at a time. These dens of iniquity catered to almost every sensual activity until the early Christian emperors banned the bathhouses in the fourth century. However, later residents of Rome would find salvation in a new use: Michelangelo adapted the main hall into a church in 1563.

The baths were also a design model for various other building types, including the great basilica of Emperor Constantine, the domed churches of the Ottoman Empire, the vaulted cathedrals of the Middle Ages, and railway stations in Europe and America.

TRIUMPHAL ARCHES

No simple black granite walls to honor heroic military campaigns. The Romans built ornate triumphal arches dating from 200 B.C. The Arch of Titus (A.D. 81), commemorating the capture of Jerusalem, has attached composite columns and relief panels depicting the emperor riding in triumph and showing off the spoils of victory. The white marble triple Arch of Septimius Severus (A.D. 203) stands in the old forum. They probably look familiar. You didn't actually think the Arch of Triumph in Paris or the structure in New York's Washington Square that provides shelter for drug dealers were originals?

START SPREADING THE NEWS

The Romans built their Empire not by friendly colonization but by sheer brute strength and military aggression. The Romans as conquerors were a practical and determined lot who excelled at administering territories, making laws, and constructing engineering masterpieces. For its subjects, Roman rule meant roads, bridges, aqueducts, sewers, and harbors, as well as baths, markets, forums, theaters, and temples for a not very exacting religion (those demands would come later with rise of the Catholic Church).

In the town of Nimes (in current southern France) stands the Maison Carree (16 B.C.), the best-preserved Roman temple in existence. Set on a 12-foot-high podium, the temple boasts a well-detailed Corinthian order and has steps only on the west entrance facade. It is called "pseudoperipteral" because the exterior colonnade is not entirely freestanding but is engaged to the cella walls along the flanks and the back.

As the Romans emerged as the mightiest people on earth,

Nimes has long been susceptible to carpetbagging architects. The Romans built Maison Carree there more than 2,000 years ago.

A MODEL FOR CHRISTIANS

In Roman days, basilicas were halls of justice, public assembly, and commercial exchange. Originally, the term indicated function, not form. The typical basilica was a large rectangular building with aisles and galleries and a semi-circular space opposite the entrance for the tribunal. These were utilitarian buildings in ancient Rome, but their form was picked up by the early followers of Jesus and became the model for their first churches. Those first zealots wanted their places of worship to look totally different from pagan religious architecture. By the fourth century, Christian basilicas pretty much had a standard form: oblong plan, longitudinal axis, a timber roof, clerestory windows, and an apse opposite the front door. The basilica was the link between Classical and Christian architecture.

powerful architectural statements were a concrete confirmation of their prowess. They built landmarks throughout their Empire and were responsible for the spread of Classicism, which became the first truly international style of architecture. Because they used the Classical idiom for their governmental and civic structures, the style became firmly associated with secular rather than religious functions. As a result, early Christians usually shunned the strict formal look of the Classical temple when they built their churches.

BYZANTINE DESIGN:
GO EAST, YOUNG ARCHITECTS

The style started about 400 years before the birth of Christ in a town called Byzantium, when it became the capital of the Roman Empire. Trouble had been brewing in the Empire during the third century, A.D. By 312, the Eastern Caesar, Constantine, had invaded Italy and captured Rome. In twelve years, he had suppressed opposition and reunited the Empire. During this period, he converted to Christianity and decided to relocate the capital to the east in a town called Constantinople. Constantine died in 337, and although he didn't live to see his namesake capital become a great metropolis, he did set its architectural tone.

Whereas Greece and Rome had temples, Constantinople had Christian churches. The granddaddy of them all is a structure called Hagia Sophia, or divine wisdom,

*From the outside, Hagia Sophia looks every bit
as massive and complex as it is.*

built as part of Constantine's initial plan for the city. It is the epitome of Byzantine architecture. In its fierce boldness, Hagia Sophia represents the antithesis of the logic of Roman architecture and of the fastidious perfectionism of the Classical Greek designs. It is an example of architecture intended not to impress but to stir one's deepest religious sentiments.

The exterior of Hagia Sophia is not overly ornate, nothing distracts from the bold form, which is essentially symmetrical, rising in semidomed modular steps to the great central dome. The monumental interior gives the impression of one vast domed space, but the detailed effect, with the great hemicycles and smaller auxiliary spaces, creates a building of unexpected intimacy.

Hagia Sophia has undergone more than its share of rebuildings and renovations, and little is known of its

BYZANTINE ROOFLINE GEOMETRY

In addition to esthetics, Byzantine architects developed some pretty nifty engineering techniques. Looking to capitalize on the Eastern mystical figure of the circle, they tackled the problem of putting a round dome over a square building. Their structural invention is called a pendentive, in which series of inverted concave triangles rise from the corners to support the dome. In a typical configuration, two side domes absorb the thrust of the main dome, while four central arches and eight main piers form a rigid, structurally independent system. This vaulting produces significantly lower thrusts requiring fewer and less muscular supports.

Building Your
Architectural Vocabulary

Mihrab: A niche or other feature of a mosque which points toward Mecca.

Mimbar: The part of the mosque where the pulpit is located.

Minaret: A slender, lofty tower attached to a mosque and surrounded by one or more projecting balconies from which the summons to prayer is cried.

Mosque: A religious building used for worship by Muslims.

Pendentive: A triangular segment of vaulting used to effect a transition at the angles from a square or polygon base to a round dome above.

earliest appearance. Although construction started in the fourth century, the Hagia Sophia we know today was begun in 532, after the earlier sanctuary was destroyed by fire. At the time, it was one of the largest and most structurally complex edifices in the world, yet it took less than five years to build. In 1453 when Constantinople fell to Islam, every icon of Christianity was stripped away.

The Muslims converted it into a mosque and added four colossal minarets. Today it's a museum. Hagia Sophia's resolve shows that the gods may come and go, but a good building, like a good cigar, is a smoke.

SUMMARY

⏱ The Romans were essentially practical builders, who borrowed unscrupulously from the earlier Etruscan cultures and later from the Greeks.

⏱ Not content to merely copy, they adapted the Classical vocabulary into their own idiom through highly sophisticated engineering feats.

⏱ With structural finesse and innovative materials, Roman builders were able to create and manipulate the largest interior spaces of all time.

⏱ They constructed portentous buildings and intricate infrastructures throughout the land. Their brand of Classicism became the trademark of the Empire, creating the first truly international style of architecture.

CHAPTER 5

EASTERN ASIA
(7000 B.C.–A.D. 1800)

YOU MUST REMEMBER THIS

Every school child knows that Asia is the largest continent, so it's only natural that it would have a lot of architecture. Three main cultures stand out. The Chinese developed a sophisticated tradition of wood construction, but their craftsmanship lacked staying power; few of their ancient buildings survive. The Japanese built to last and managed to preserved more of their architectural heritage in spite of attacks by everything from barbaric tribes to atomic bombs. In India, the Hindus and Buddhists focused on constructing monuments to their gods.

MOST FAMOUS FOR

★ The Great Wall of China (fifth to second centuries B.C.; reconstructed regularly through the fifteenth and sixteenth centuries A.D.)
★ Forbidden City in Beijing (A.D. 1406–1420)
★ Angkor Wat, Cambodia (A.D. 1112–1152)
★ The Great Stupa at Sanchi, or its less glamorous moniker Stupa No. 1 (first century B.C.)
★ Taj Mahal, Agra, India (A.D. 1630–1653)

TAKE A RIDE ON THE
ORIENT EXPRESS

O ther civilizations have come and gone, but China keeps on trucking. Four thousand years ago, the people of the Far East were building a society that has continued longer than any other in recorded history. Unfortunately, its ancient architecture hasn't held up so well. Archeological finds, excavated pottery models, and written records indicate a tradition of sophisticated wooden buildings with post-and-lintel construction, ingenious bracketing systems, and elabo-

---

· Building Your
Achitectural Vocabulary

Feng shui: The Chinese practice that prescribes the proper placement of all doors and windows to ensure good fortune for the inhabitants (very popular today in L.A.—and why not?—what with all those earthquakes, droughts, floods, fires, and riots, not to mention sensational murders).

Hosho: The crowning sacred gem on a pagoda.

Tou-kung: System of bracketing, evolved over many centuries. It let each pillar support a larger area, which in turn enabled builders to increase the spacing between the outer row of pillars supporting the building.

rate rooflines of overhangs and upturned eaves. But few buildings exist in China predating the Ming Dynasty (A.D. 1368–1644). You can fault war and barbaric inva-sions, but most of the blame lies with their choice of materials: rammed earth, wood, and partitions of plaster, rice paper, matting, or lattice—not exactly a system of construction expected to last for a couple of millennia. Although few of their buildings are around to be tourist attractions today, they did meet the needs of their users (esthetics and permanence aside, that's still a noble role of architecture).

BIG FENCES MAKE GOOD NEIGHBORS

One venerable vestige of ancient China does survive: the aptly named Great Wall. Winding more than 2,000 miles along China's northern mountains, this ancient rampart would stretch from Washington, D.C., to beyond Denver, Colorado. That's a long schlepp. But the Wall, like Rome, wasn't built in a day.

Following the period of the Warring States (fifth–third centuries B.C.), Shin-Huang Ti came to power as the First Emperor by uniting the Empire in 221 B.C.. In addition to burning books and setting up an oppressive regime, Shin pieced together a haphazard chain of fortifications, which had been built over the previous three centuries, to create an unbroken wall.

In many aspects, the Great Wall resembles Hadrian's Wall, which runs between Scotland and England. Like its Western counterpart, China's grandiose barrier fol-lows the contour of the landscape, with beacon towers, gates, and ramp approaches placed at regular intervals.

The Great Wall of China has stood 2,000-plus years longer than the Berlin Wall and shows no signs of falling.

The Great Wall proved to be of little value for defense, but it did create boundaries for a unified China and a system of transportation and communication.

SQUARE PEG IN A ROUND WHOLE

The Chinese believed the earth to be a stable cube set in a circular universe. This set the standard for a square society in the design of cities, ceremonial buildings, palaces, as well as modest residences. Towns were organized with geometric precision with streets at right angles, oriented south-north and west-east. The main gateway into town always faced the south, which signified warmth and goodness.

Beijing, with its rectangular city plan, embodies these ideas. Anchoring the southern terminus of the city's main avenue is a large courtyard called Daqingmen, the gateway to the inner city of Beijing. Continuing along the axis is the T-shaped Tiananmen Square (popular gathering spot even today).

At the center of this elaborate town plan stands the fortified royal palace, the Forbidden City. Most of the luxurious residences of the emperors were destroyed upon the fall of their dynasties—only the Forbidden City is preserved intact. Although construction began on the Forbidden City in bits and pieces as early as the fifth century, the complex was built in earnest from 1406 to 1420. Today it's a museum. And what a great stage set it provides for all those epic Chinese movies involving

THE ORIGINAL GARDEN PARTY

The various Chinese religions influenced diverse aspects of design. The Daoists were sorta like the religious "Green Party" of the day. Less militant than today's environmental fanatics, the Daoists extolled the virtues of a harmonious relationship with the land and respect for the laws of nature. They glorified the landscape through poetry and paintings, and established the tradition of Chinese garden architecture. On the downside, they are probably responsible for all those suburban rock gardens with flowing water and plastic pagoda birdbaths.

For sheer grandeur, you can't beat the Forbidden City.

little princes and buddhas, not to mention real-life hero-
ics with students facing down tanks.

Within the Forbidden City's confines are a slew of sacred halls honoring such lofty goals as supreme harmony, central harmony, preserved harmony, literary
glory, martial valor, celestial purity, and terrestrial union.
The largest of the sacred halls is the Hall of Taihedian.
Set on a three-tiered terrace surrounded by an ornate

marble balustrade, the hall has a roof with double eaves and glazed yellow tiles, and is animated with carved dragons and phoenixes. Twenty-four Chinese emperors over nearly 500 years lived in and ruled from the Forbidden City.

ON THE EAVE AND A PRAYER

As Buddhism spread through China, temples starting appearing on the landscape. The earliest Buddhist temples comprised a symbolic tower with a temple hall. Later Buddhist compounds had various buildings arranged around courtyards. But it is the pagoda that characterizes the Buddhist temple in China, as well as a lot of tacky Chinese restaurants around the U.S. More than 2,000 pagodas still stand in China. One of the oldest remaining pagodas—although it's nearly in ruins—is the Songyue Temple, built in the early sixth century. Rising 131 feet, the pagoda is a twelve-sided tower with an octagonal interior.

The Chinese built shrines not only to their many gods, but to ancestors and other rich and famous historical personalities. One of the most reknowned collections of sacred buildings is the Tiantan Shrine complex, which covers more than 690 acres in the southern district of Beijing. One cluster of buildings is the Qiniandian, which includes the 106-foot-tall circular wooden Hall of Prayer. Reflecting the Chinese flair for color, the Hall of Prayer has a triple conical roof clad with deep blue glazed tiles and is crowned with a large gold-plated ball. The Tiantan Shrine complex also includes the Huanqiutan, a three-tiered circular marble terrace. Ornate marble balustrades surround each tier. A single-roofed circular structure, the Huangquiongyu (or Imperial Vault of Heaven) is located prominently within a circular courtyard.

SHANGRI-LA OR JUST YOUR TYPICAL ABSOLUTE PREACHER'S MODEST MANSE

Depending on your point of view, the Potala Palace in Lhasa, Tibet, is either a most holy place or just another monument to religious extremism. Constructed in the latter part of the seventeenth century, the compound is made up of the White Palace, the Red Palaces, and the ornate Golden Palace, which features three wooden-framed roofs inlaid with golden tiles and surrounded by five towers covered in gold leaf. It was the center of Tibetan Buddhism before the Chinese occupied Tibet in 1951. The Dalai Lama still maintains that it's his rightful home.

ISLANDS IN A STREAM AND ON A FAULT LINE

The Japanese archipelago was virtually isolated from the Western world until the second half of the nineteenth century. Architectural and other influences came primarily from China and India via the Korean peninsula. Japan, like China, was well forested, and its abundant rainfall assured great quantities of excellent timber. Quality stone for building was not readily available, and even if it had been plentiful, the hazards of earthquakes discouraged its use. (To paraphrase the NRA, earthquakes don't kill people, buildings do.) As a result, the Japanese developed meticulous techniques of wooden construction.

Mother Nature had some influence on the evolution of Japan's architecture. But as with most societies, religion was the divine force that shaped the built environment. Most of the country's oldest structures have some type of holy function. By the fourth century, the Shinto religion, which venerates the landscape and all things natural, had emerged as the predominant faith. The holiest Shinto shrines are located at Ise. In the beginning this sacred site was probably distinguished only by an entrance gateway (*torii*) and a simple fence (*tamagaki*). As religious sacraments developed, the deities were given physical forms, and shrines were built to welcome the gods for their sojourns on earth.

At Ise, they set the design standards and traditions. All the shrine buildings feature an elevated floor set on columns embedded in the earth instead of set on stone foundations. The wood used for the framework of posts, beams, and rafters was an indigenous white cypress, which was stripped of bark and planed smooth. A custom developed in which every twenty years the shrine would be demolished and rebuilt with a replica of the old shrine. This tradition, called *shikinen-sengu,* ensured that each generation would transmit to posterity not only the religious ceremonies but the art of building. The present shrine at Ise was rebuilt in 1993 with old-fashioned technology, and could pass for 1,300 years old.

By the end of the seventh century, Buddhism supplanted Shinto as the state religion. The construction of the Todai-ji Monastery, founded in 745, helped to mark the occasion. The original buildings were lost to natural disasters and fire, but without missing a beat, lost structures were replicated, sometimes as exact copies, other times with slight alterations. The Todai-ji Daibutsuden Hall, or Hall of the Great Buddha, has been rebuilt twice in its history. And although today's version is smaller than the eighth-century original, at 187 feet by 164 feet, it is still one of the largest hand-built wooden buildings in the world.

NOT JUST FOR THE GODS

In addition to temples, the Japanese a thousand years ago were building some pretty nifty secular structures. Kyoto was established as the capital at the start of the Heian period (794–1185) and was laid out with a grid of streets, square lots, and a broad south-north avenue. The original Imperial Palace in Kyoto was destroyed by fire in 1227, and over the next several hundred years a series of royal structures were built on the site. The current Shishinden at the Imperial Palace, which accommodated royal ceremonies, was rebuilt in 1855.

While the aristocracy of Kyoto was absorbed in the cult of beauty and the arts, life in the hinterlands from the sixteenth to seventeenth centuries was not always a bed of chrysanthemums. Civil wars raged, and feudal lords were building massive stone castles set atop pedestals and surrounded by moats and a maze of earthen ramparts. The most impressive and best preserved of the fortified residences of this not-so-peaceful period is the Himeji Castle in Himeji City, built between 1601 and 1614. These sudden stylistic innovations were in response to the introduction of artillery during the civil wars, and defensibility rather than esthetics spawned the complexities of approach and plan.

INDIA: THE JEWEL IN THE CROWN

The history of India is long and tangled. In terms of architecture, it is nearly impossible to trace a neat, orderly development. In India, as in many countries, religion did and still does shape the built environment as well as influence the political order. The complex threads of the region's social history bind its architectural evolution.

The first known buildings in southern Asia date from the third century B.C. and relate to Buddhism and Jainism. Later came Hinduism around the time the Western calendar changed from B.C. to A.D. The next stylistic wave, which lasted from the beginning of the thirteenth century until the middle of the eighteenth century, came with the Muslim conquest—an exotic twist on Islamic architecture tailored to India. Then came two hundred years of British rule with their conservative Colonial style, and finally there was Modernism.

DON'T CALL ME STUPA

The most outstanding examples of ancient Indian architecture are the stupas. Originating as prehistoric burial mounds, the earliest stupas held the remains of holy men or nobles. Later, chambers were added to intern sacred relics of the Buddha. A rounded canopy was set above the mound to add a mark of distinction, and this umbrella form evolved to take the shape of a cone, which is known as a *chatravalli*.

One of the oldest extant stupas (and still looking good after 2,000 years of hard praying) is the Great Stupa at Sanchi, sometimes called Stupa No. 1, which dates from the first century B.C. and is located in central India.

THE LABYRINTH THAT IS INDIA; THE MOSAIC THAT IS INDONESIA

Buddhism also spread eastward. On the Indonesian island of Java, against a backdrop of smoking volcanoes, stands the magnificent Stupa of Barabudur like a shallow stone-clad hill packed full of symbolism. The lower five receding terraces, 500-foot square in plan at the base, represent life on earth. The upper three circular terraces portray heaven and support seventy-two individual stupas, each with its own statue of Buddha facing outward. The crowning central stupa symbolizes "eternal truth." The gallery corridors display more than 1,300 panels of elaborate sculptures telling the life and times of Buddha. The organization, orientation, and ornamentation of this spectacular piece of work were dictated by religious ideas rather than design principles, proving again that preachers make pretty good architectural practitioners.

FORM FOLLOWS KARMA

Buddhism wasn't the only game in town. India is also home to Jainism and has rock-cut shrines dating from the third century B.C. Later Jain temples were traditional

*The Great Stupa shows some of the earliest efforts at
transferring techniques of wood carving to stone. It features
magnificent sculptures in the round and in relief
on the stone fences that surround the compound.*

stone buildings, usually crowned with a dome and a spire
and introduced with a pillared portico in the form of an
octagon set within a square. In contrast to the more
subdued Buddhist architecture, the Jainists, as well as the
Hindus, loved to accessorize and pile up ornamentation—often drawing inspiration from human and animal
forms in sensual poses.

One well-known Jain complex is Pilitana, which sits
atop the twin peaks of the sacred Satrunjaya hill and
the Kathiawar peninsula in Gujerat. Scores of temples of
varying sizes, built over hundreds of years starting in the
eleventh century, make up the compound.

THEY DON'T GET MUCH BIGGER

Among India's religions, however, it was the Hindus who gradually rose to prominence. And they built some impressive sacred spots. From the eighth century until the nineteenth century when the Western influences began to shape Indian architecture, Hindu dynasties maintained political power and design clout. For Hindu building programs, there were official manuals, called *sastras,* about siting, methods of construction, materials, exterior finishes, and configurations to please different gods. The Hindu temple, like its counterpart in ancient Greece, was a dwelling place of the gods, not a place intended for congregational use by mere mortals.

Pilgrims to Angkor Wat had better wear their walking shoes—the comprehensive tour winds more than 13 miles.

The Hindus build thousands of temples throughout India and expanded their religious hold east through Burma into Thailand and Cambodia. Hindu architecture reached its apex in Southeast Asia with the construction of Angkor Wat (1112–1152) in Cambodia. One of the largest religious complexes in the world, Angkor Wat is a giant rectangle contained by a moat 2.5 miles long. Its form is a familiar stepped pyramid, with the third and final level supporting the most sacred sanctuary, which is crowned by a monumental conical tower. Four smaller towers anchor each of the corners of the great platform.

DON'T FORGET THE MUSLIMS

Another exotic variety of architecture arose in India with the Muslim conquest, beginning in the tenth century. The first mosques, built in Delhi and Ajmer in the twelfth century, displayed elements of Hindu and Jain temples but with a decidedly Islamic stance. These early Muslim buildings incorporated such features as arcaded porticoes, minarets, pointed arches, free stucco work, and floral patterns set in a geometrical framework.

The creation of the Mogul Empire in the mid-sixteenth century brought on another round of splendid eclectic architecture. The greatest period of building followed the accession of Akbar, son of Humayun, to power. The apex of Akbar's building program was the new royal town of Fatehpur Sikri, constructed from 1569 to 1580. Set on a hilltop site, the city was deserted by the court because of the difficulty in supplying water to the growing population. The palace, congregational mosque, and other structures survive in a virtually unaltered state.

Like other ancient civilizations, Indians devoted excessive energy on monuments to the dead, such as the Tomb of Humayun (he was the father of Akbar) in Delhi. Built in 1556, the burial compound sits in a for-

A GIFT TO DIE FOR

Forget the jewels, the furs, and the BMW. You know your man really loves you if he gives you the Taj Mahal. Emperor Shad Jahan built this exquisite tomb for his favorite consort, Mumtaz Mahal. The Taj Mahal sits on a 313-foot square terrace and casts a great reflection in the central canal. Four minarets rise to 137 feet to anchor each corner but are scaled to accentuate the effect of the dominant, if slightly bulbous, dome.

The Taj Mahal is one of the most photogenic buildings in the world.

mal garden intersected by a grid of canals and pathways. It stands on a massive red sandstone foundation anchored with four octagonal towers that support a marble double-shelled dome. With its massive stature, bold ornamentation, and strong massing, the tomb did much to popularize the more purely Islamic style and set a high standard for honoring the dead.

SUMMARY

Hundreds, if not thousands, of cultures exist in Asia and there's almost as many architectural influences shaping this vast and complex land.

The religious architecture of China and Japan evolved more slowly than any other architecture in history. But few of their ancient buildings survive.

The Hindu and Buddhist shrines of the Far East were not intended to be monuments to the achievement of mortals. Their sole purpose and their forms were dictated by the ritual needs of religion, not the egos of preachers.

Religion and politics: you aren't supposed to talk about either at cocktail parties, but you'd be hard pressed to sound informed about Asian architecture unless you mention both.

CHAPTER 6

ANCIENT MESOAMERICA AND PERU
(1200 B.C.–A.D. 1500)

YOU MUST REMEMBER THIS

From the first millennium B.C. to the sixteenth century when uninvited Spaniards arrived, cultures from central Mexico southward through Central America and down to Peru were building colossal pyramids, splendid temples, grand cities, and elaborate infrastructures. These great civilizations rivaled the architectural achievements of Egypt and Mesopotamia, but the ancient peoples of the Americas developed "in situ," without knowledge of what was happening across the Atlantic. All their built marvels were constructed without the benefits of the wheel, iron tools, or a standard of weights and measures.

MOST FAMOUS FOR

★ Teotihuacán (250 B.C.–A.D. 650)
★ The Temple of the Giant Jaguar at Tikal (c. A.D. 500)
★ The Palace of the Governors, (c. A.D. 900)
★ Chichén Itzá (A.D. 1000–1200)
★ Machu Picchu (c. A.D. 1500)

SOUTH OF THE BORDER, DOWN MEXICO WAY

The Americas were inhabited by humans later than other parts of the globe, but that hadn't kept the New World from incubating some great ancient civilizations. The city of Teotihuacán, which had its heyday around 1,800 years ago, rivals the grandest urban ensembles of the ancient world—Giza, Persepolis, Athens, Rome. The development of a social hierarchy is also a match for any of the other ancient sovereignties. The class structure of the Mesoamerican cultures was based on an omnipotent ruling priesthood, supported by large peasant and slave populations. Looking back through history—no matter what continent we're on—it seems that the more tyrannical the preachers, popes, and kings, the better their architecture.

Like any respectable high civilization, the Mesoameri-

A CIVILIZATION BY ANY OTHER NAME WOULD SMELL AS SWEET

These civilizations used to be called pre-Columbian, but the politically correct name is now Mesoamerican for regions of Central America (*meso,* you'll recall, is Greek for "middle"). Unfortunately, the new and improved name doesn't technically include Peru, which was home to the Incas. Another name that is used sometimes is pre-Hispanic, but that only replaces Christopher Columbus with another "Eurocencratic" adjective. And in fact, the Spanish invaders did much more damage to the neighborhood than Columbus ever did.

can societies mastered agriculture, established religions, and developed systems of writing, mathematics, astronomy, and calendars. Reading, 'riting, and 'rithmetic are impressive achievements in the jungle, but even Mesoamerica wouldn't rate a mention in this book unless its peoples had created their own architectural language. Which they did—their unique twist on the enduring pyramid form. At first glance, these Middle American stepped compositions resemble the graded pyramid of Saqqâra or the ziggurats of Mesopotamia, but in form and function there are big differences—like providing altars for human sacrifice. In terms of appearance, the

MULTICULTURAL BEFORE MULTICULTURAL WAS COOL

This was a land of many diverse peoples who established different societies and found distinctive creative outlets. The Olmecs were the earliest and laid a foundation (literally, since many of their ruins were later built upon) for later civilizations. From that society developed the great Maya culture, which is often divided in three cleverly named periods: pre-Classic, before A.D. 100; Classic, 100 to 900; and post-Classic, 900 to 1525. That the Maya had a talent for craftsmanship, architectural ornament, and fine proportions is evident in the hundreds of monumental structures that survive today.

The Aztecs and the Toltecs were the fighters, and their monuments celebrated these aggressive tendencies. In the Toltec city of Tula, 15-foot-tall columns carved to resemble warriors support the roof of the major temple. The Aztecs were latecomers but rose distinctions are slightly more subtle—minor details like materials, orientation, pitch of pyramid walls, stairways, and esthetics of ornamentation.

Mesoamerica's grand architectural achievements are all the more remarkable because these ancient peoples had neither the pulley system nor the wheel. They understood post-and-lintel construction, but they never learned how to build an arch. (It's unexplainable how or why some civilizations excelled in certain areas and then never caught on to other relatively simple concepts. It's like why one kid will do well in language, while another will ace math.)

(***continued***)
. . . .
quickly. They were less focused on architecture than on matters of the heart-finding prisoners for the sacred ritual of ripping out the still-beating organs of the condemned. Few of their structures survive. Their ancient capital, Tenochtitlán, was burned to the ground in 1521 by the Spanish. Its sacred center now lies buried under Mexico City.

There were other less-publicized societies, which had smaller geographical coverage and diminished longevity, that also made contributions to the architectural heritage, like the Zapotecs, who built a great mountain-top city in the Oaxaca region.

The Incas were master builders and engineers, constructing great metropolises and evolving a complex infrastructure of bridges and roads high in the Peruvian Andes.

BUILDING A FOUNDATION

The earliest Mesoamerican peoples, the Olmecs, sprang up along the Gulf of Mexico a couple of millennia before Christ. They extended their influence into central Mexico and as far south as modern Guatemala. The Olmecs are credited for building the first planned architectural entities on the American continent—extraordinary ceremonial centers. The earliest of these ritualistic complexes were comprised of terraces and platforms of packed earth and clay bricks. The materials were simple, but these centers possessed a calculated symmetry with elevated and recessed plazas and a distinct orientation based on their designers' knowledge of astronomy. Principal buildings and monumental sculptures were set in a line to create a formal axis.

The most important structure at these ceremonial centers was the pyramid temple. A close second was the ball court. Their ball games had spiritual overtones, which is not unlike present-day America where sports are a religion for many. Our games are still played on the Sabbath, with really big events reserved for high holidays. But their stakes were even bigger than the Super Bowl or the World Series. Winning really *was* everything because the losers were often massacred—grisly rituals more horrifying than the stampedes at World Cup soccer matches.

WITH A LOCATION TO DIE FOR

The most important harbinger of architecture to come was the Temple Pyramid at Cuicuilco (c. 500 B.C.). Constructed of adobe reinforced with large stones, this great circular structure featured a stepped base with a diameter of approximately 492 feet and rose to a height of 150 feet. The original pyramid's two stages were later enlarged to four, with ramps and stairways along the east and west facades. Cuicuilco was an important center but suffered a nasty natural disaster: The volcano Xitli erupted twenty or so centuries ago, burying the whole southwest region of the Valley of Mexico.

BRIGHT LIGHTS, BIG CITY

After the volcano, these first Middle Americans decided to relocate to growing new cities like Tlapacoya, Tikal, and Teotihuacán. The most sophisticated of these urban centers was Teotihuacán, which flourished from approximately 250 B.C. to A.D. 650, and was home to a number of early and overlapping societies. Its name means "the place where those who die become gods," which may have to do with the fact that the town hosted regular human sacrifices. After its decline as a thriving metropolis, the Aztecs continued to use the ceremonial center as a burial spot for VIPs up until the sixteenth century.

Teotihuacán was laid out in a traditional grid pattern of streets and covered more than 13 square miles. Its population peaked at more than 150,000 people. The ancient city of Teotihuacán was larger than Imperial Rome. (Think of the tax base.) A broad avenue, lined with a series of ceremonial buildings, ran through the heart of downtown. The largest was the Pyramid of the Sun, rising to a height of more than 215 feet. Built over the course of five centuries, from about 200 B.C. to A.D. 300, it was located along the east side of the central boulevard cleverly named "the street of the dead." No contemporary Chamber of Commerce would understand the appeal this name held for the inhabitants of the time. A sweeping flight of stairs rises along the west facade, aligned with the setting sun on summer solstice (that's June 22, the first day of summer, in case you didn't remember). The stone-faced pyramid ascends in four stages and used to be crowned with a small temple-like structure.

Facing the Sun Pyramid is a large open plaza with clusters of cell-like residences surrounding small sunken courtyards. Although these residences were relatively modest, they featured portico-type entrances with paired columns—like today's tacky suburban builder-houses that boast an overscaled columned front porch.

Anchoring the northern end of the "street of the dead" was the Moon Pyramid, the sun's smaller compan-

*Teotihuacán was a great city with the mammoth
Pyramid of the Sun and a well-defined "street of the dead."*

ion but equally sacred. The complex is also home to the
pyramid of the powerful god Quetzalcóatl, the Plumed
Serpent. The town's Citadel, which was built several centuries after the Sun and Moon pyramids, is today a large
grassy court surrounded on three sides by terraced platforms with the different levels separated by deep strongly
framed friezes.

Any religious shrine attracts its share of pilgrims and
wackos, and Teotihuacán was no exception. It became a
center for trade, and the city featured a vast marketplace
across the road from the Citadel and numerous mom-
and-pop variety shops around town selling souvenirs.

WITH A EMPHASIS ON THE FINER THINGS OF LIFE

In the Toltec capital city of Tula, the emphasis was on art and sculpture. Sure, they built a grand five-stage pyramid, but it was their decorators, not their engineers, who broke new ground. Colossal carved figures holding a bag of incense and a deadly spear served as columns for the main temple. A pair of cylindrical columns detailed with feathered serpents flanked the entrance. Stone panels cladding the buildings featured jaguars, coyotes, and best of all, eagles eating human hearts. (Do you think a local

GO TELL IT ON THE MOUNTAIN

Monte Albán, the temple city of the Zapotecs in the Oaxaca region, might not be the most sophisticated ceremonial center in terms of architecture but it sure has a great view. Here the important religious structures were clustered atop a mountain crest overlooking three broad valleys. The rest of the city's more mundane functions were located on the slopes below. Unlike builders who just want to copy what's popular in the next city, the designers of Monte Albán chose to be a little more site specific. They appreciated their mountaintop, so they focused on the relationship between the structures and open spaces in order to take advantage of the view. Many buildings featured flat roofs supported by columns. The center's wide stairways and broad balustrades were never matched in the ancient Western Hemisphere. The Great Plaza is also decidedly different, shaped somewhat like an arrowhead rather than a simple rectangle or square.

artist would have had trouble getting an NEA grant for that one?)

CLASS ACTION

In southern Mexico and down into Central America where the Maya peoples were forming urban centers, the city of Tikal was settled in a slightly different fashion. It was unabashedly elitist. Only the rich folks got to live downtown; the lesser sorts were relegated to the suburbs. But every now and then, the poor relations got the chance to go "uptown" for the religious shindigs. One look at the Temple of the Giant Jaguar at Tikal was usually enough to make the little people forget their troubles. Built around the fifth century A.D., this temple pyramid is a superb example of Classic Maya architecture. The structure rises in ten stages to a height of approximately 156 feet. Each platform is separated by almost vertical walls that give the building a monumental, towering stance. Perched on top is the temple proper.

MAIZEY, HOT, AND HUMID

The Yucatán Peninsula is hot and muggy and has poor soil, but here some of the best efforts in Maya architecture arose beginning somewhere around the first or second century A.D., peaking by 1000. One of the most beautiful cities of the region is Uxmal. Clean proportions and restraint were the architectural watchwords of local designers. The town boasts a sophisticated grouping of

(*continued*)
....

eight important buildings, with the Palace of the Governors getting top billing. The palace consists of a large
central building flanked with two identical wings, which
were originally connected by hallways whose vaults
were the tallest built by the Maya culture. Decorative
carvings adorn the heavily sculpted frieze set above a
plain stone-walled ground floor.

An important component of Uxmal is the Nunnery, an
assemblage of elongated buildings arranged around a
spacious courtyard, with the corners left open. (That's
its name even though it was hundreds of years before
the Catholic Church sent its emissaries.) The grouping
is open and airy, much less compact than the acropolis-
type building arrangements that were common throughout central Mexico.

Don't Call Me Chicken

Chichén Itzá's development hatched during the Classic
Mayan period around the eighth to ninth centuries A.D.
and continued more than six hundred years into the
later Toltec era. The buildings of the town reflect the
influences of both peoples—the more relaxed Mayas and
the decidedly uptight Toltecs, the warring tribe who
thrived on human sacrifice and destruction. In spite of
these minor personality flaws, the Toltecs were great
builders. Here in Chichén Itzá we find the first break
with the Yucatán Peninsula's established design traditions and the development of a new cultural and architectural vocabulary.

One of the city's most impressive structures is the Temple of the Warriors and the nearby Court of the Thousand Columns. The main approach to the temple is through a colonnade of square columns leading to a single broad stairway. Exterior facades are decorated with projecting trunk-like forms associated with the long-nosed Maya rain god.

FIELD OF SCREAMS

No trip to town would be complete without a visit to the ballpark, and Chichén Itzá had a humdinger. Measuring 550 feet in length, this extravaganza is the largest of Mesoamerica's 500-plus ball courts that have been discovered. The grassy playing field is flanked by high walls elaborately detailed with intertwined replicas of those ubiquitous plumed serpents. A stone bench running along the base of the walls shows carved bas-relief scenes from past games. Guaranteed to keep the players on their toes, the selected highlights depict the sacrifice of losing players by decapitation—always the perfect "grand finale" in a friendly game of sport.

Another architectural landmark at Chichén Itzá is El Castillo, a temple pyramid with awesome stairways rising on all four sides to an ornate rooftop sanctuary. Dedicated to the ever-popular plumed serpent god, Quetzalcóatl, the monument features carved snakes everywhere. The town also had a great observatory; those hot-headed Toltecs liked to look at the stars when they weren't waging war.

MOCTEZUMA'S REVENGE

If you spent the first three days of your Cancun vacation in the bathroom, you don't need anyone to describe this phenomenon. For those of you who didn't drink the water, here's the straight poop.

In 1519 a bad-ass Spaniard named Hernan Cortés hit the Aztec capital city of Tenochtitlán and found a sophisticated walled urban enclave with temples, pyramids, a royal palace, a ballpark, and downtown housing. The Aztecs, led at the time by Moctezuma II, were defeated in short order, but not before they destroyed their own hometown so there would be no spoils for the victors. Today Mexico City sits atop the ruins. Some say Moctezuma took Cortés to be the reincarnated god Quetzalcóatl, and that he believed his mere Aztec mortals didn't have a chance. Cortés's horses, armor, gunpowder, artillery, and infantry might have also had something to do with the outcome.

Now this revered ruler is a mere mention in the history books, but his avenging spirit, people say, continues to live in infamy in the intestines of modern-day tourists to Mexico.

CLIMB EVERY MOUNTAIN

The landscape of Peru is very different from that of Central America, and this shows in its architecture. The great Andes mountain range rises about 60 miles east of the Pacific Ocean. The narrow north-south coastal strip is arid; the mountain region is some of the wildest and most desolate terrain in the world. Not exactly conducive to a fledging civilization, but relatively advanced societies have existed in the neighborhood for more than 3,500 years. Like their contemporaries in Mesoamerica, the societies of Peru never invented the wheel, but they did domesticate the native, and relatively lazy, llama (pronounced *Ya-ma*) for farm work. They also wove some great alpaca sweaters from the wool of that mountain mammal.

By A.D. 600, Tiahuanaco in the southern highlands was booming. A political and religious powerhouse, Tiahuanaco was home to the Gate of the Sun, a monumental gateway to a impressive ceremonial site. Cut from a single block, the sculpture features a rectangular opening emphasized with a recessed band and topped with an ornate frieze with a formalized image of the god Viracocha.

Six centuries later, Chanchan, the capital of the Chimu Empire, boasted an urban precinct measuring six miles square and encompassing ten large compounds, each enclosed by 30-foot-tall walls. Forts were also a popular outlet for architectural achievements. The Fortress at Paramonga is one of the best of these defensive compounds. Successive terraces and fortified walls are arranged to defend the lower sections, and corner bastions protect the main ramparts.

Other societies developed later up and down the coast. But nothing compared with the Incas, who from about 1200 to 1530 ruled the roost. The Incas started out as a small sovereignty in the town of Cuzco at the beginning of the thirteenth century, and they soon expanded their empire over much of Ecuador and south through Bolivia and into parts of Argentina and northern Chile.

Cuzco's tasteful downtown featured numerous well-built masonry structures and a central plaza where the leading temple stood. Remnants of the temple's curved wall, finished in ashlar masonry (that's smooth square stones with regular courses), still exist. The Incas also constructed impressive fortresses. In the second half of the fifteenth century, more than 30,000 local laborers, using the most primitive tools, built a massive fort to defend the holy city of Cuzco. Known as the fortress of Saqsaywaman, the ancient edifice was also used for religious and royal functions. It featured three tiers with a high retaining wall of limestone that stretched for more than 1,500 feet.

LOCATION, LOCATION, LOCATION

Of numerous grand Inca cities, no place matched the physical drama of Machu Picchu. A fortress city dramatically sited above the Urubamba Gorge, Machu Picchu consists of a sophisticated assemblage of sacred plazas, temples, and houses all clinging to the steep, terraced mountainside. These were rooms with a view! Although the city now lies in ruins, extensive foundations show that buildings were constructed of local stone and incorporated trapezoidal doorways and windows. Some structures possess their original masonry gables, and stone stairways still link terraced gardens.

At the same time, these industrious Incas were also investing in their infrastructure. They constructed the Inca Royal Road of the Andes, a 3,250-mile-long highway passing through terrain as challenging as anywhere on

*Machu Picchu was an engineering marvel
perched high in the Andes.*

earth. Until the nineteenth century, it was the longest
arterial road ever built. Gorges and rivers were spanned
by sophisticated suspension and cantilevered bridges.
("Suspension" is where the bridge is hung from cables
anchored at either end and supported by towers at set
intervals; "cantilevered" means it juts out real far without visible means of support.)

But by 1532, there was trouble in paradise, and the
empire's fall from glory was decidedly quicker than its
ascent. Another aggressive Spanish explorer—this one
named Pizarro—brought the Incas to their knees in a
matter of months.

The Spanish conquistadors were impressed with the

architectural achievements of the native peoples of the New World—and not without reason. The magnificent buildings, formal city planning, and grand avenues of the Renaissance were just making their debut in Europe. Unfortunately, the invaders' awe for good design didn't slow down the rape and pillage of great civilizations.

SUMMARY

⏱ For thousands of years, civilizations flourished in the lands of Central and South America, where various societies built hundreds of architectural wonders that stand today.

⏱ Without benefit of today's global communications, these early Americans constructed temple pyramids, remarkably similar in physical appearance to the monumental structures of Egypt and the Near East.

⏱ Their great metropolis, Teotihuacán, prospered at the same time as Imperial Rome and matched its size.

⏱ These diverse societies left varied contributions: the Mayas mastered decoration, proportion, and esthetics; the Incas were the creators of great engineering feats—a 3,250-mile-long road with cantilevered and suspension bridges, for one.

CHAPTER 7

ROMANESQUE
(1000–1200)

YOU MUST REMEMBER THIS

Coined in the nineteenth century, the term Romanesque is, depending on whom you ask, either a bold, robust style that gave the world some magnificent churches or a crude prelude to the glories of Gothic architecture. It arose from the chaos of the Dark Ages of Europe and with the help of some zealous preachers spread throughout the Continent. Common characteristics: Ornament was not applied as an afterthought, but was derived from the muscular lines of the actual structure. Furthermore, Romanesque churches reach for the sky, as opposed to the long, low stance of the early Christian basilicas that hug the landscape.

MOST FAMOUS FOR

★ St. Michael's Cathedral, Hildesheim, Germany (1001–1033)
★ Cathedral and Leaning Tower of Pisa, Italy (1063–1272)
★ The Church of St. Etienne, Caen, France (1068–1115)
★ Durham Cathedral, England (1093–1133)

WHY ROMANESQUE CAN BE A CONFUSING-ESQUE TERM

Romanesque literally means "in the Roman manner," and describes the derivatives of Roman architecture that evolved in western Europe between the collapse of the Empire and the rise of Gothic designs (the next major style to emerge in western Europe, which picked up and refined many of the Romanesque features).

But the Romanesque name is misleading. Although there are affinities linking it to Rome, the style is an aggregation of diverse influences from the Byzantine and Ottoman empires to the Vikings and Celtics who were roaming around Europe (not the ones playing sports in the United States).

BURLY PRESENCE IN A BARBARIC WORLD

The brawny churches of the Romanesque movement evolved from the need to provide bigger and more impressive edifices for the swelling Christian congregations throughout the land. The church was the only game in town—no movies, no baseball, no printing presses, no restaurants, no nothing except maybe a little raping and pillaging on a big weekend.

Romanesque architecture didn't appear overnight. The movement was a "learning style" in a period of design transition marked by trial and error. And once the thousandth anniversary of Jesus Christ passed without major incident (i.e. no end of the world, no second

Building Your
Architectural Vocabulary

Bay: The portion of a building contained between adjacent piers or columns. And then there's the ever-popular bay window—that's one that projects outward from the main wall.

Idiom: A language or form of artistic expression peculiar to a people, class, or area.

Indigenous: Native to a particular region or environment.

Pier: It's a place to go fishing, but in terms of architecture it's an upright structural support at the end of an arch or a lintel. It can be freestanding or part of a wall.

Rib: A transverse or diagonal structural member of an arched vaulting.

Vault: The part of a building roofed by arched masonry.

coming), the cautious clergy of the Catholic Church were more willing to invest in real estate.

The Romanesque movement flourished in the regions that were to become France, Italy, Spain, England, and Germany. The locals put their own twist on the theme, incorporating copious regional idioms and using indigenous materials. But some common characteristics emerged—muscular masonry construction with fat molded piers and semicircular arches; sparse decoration with linear ornamentation directly derived from the line of the actual structure; and tall naves with multiple bays and cross ribbing.

Romanesque churches aren't shy or unassuming. Their towers reach for the heavens. These churches had

---

Building Your Architectural Vocabulary

Apse: Semicircular or multisided recess at the end of the sanctuary, first applied to a Roman basilica.

Baptistery: A separate building in the complex that contains a font for the christening ritual. Rural Southern Baptists usually settle for a nearby creek or pond.

Campanile: Italian term for the bell tower, generally freestanding.

Chancel: The space at the front of the church reserved for the clergy, containing the altar and choir.

Choir: A group of people who like to sing. In terms of architecture, it's the part of the church where a larger purpose than merely honoring God. They were the physical manifestation of Christian ambition. Pilgrimages and crusades were the order of the day, and monks and bishops were about the only people who could read or write, not to mention preserve knowledge about science, art, and medicine. So the construction of impressive churches was tangible and effective propaganda for the Christian order of things: a bastion of stability against a backdrop of what was basically anarchy.

(continued)

they sit when they're singing. Normally in the west part of the chancel, but in medieval churches the choir often sat beneath or west of the crossing.

Crossing: Area at the intersection of nave, chancel, and transepts in a cruciform church.

Cruciform: Simply, "in the shape of a cross."

Lantern: A windowed tower or turret corning a cupola or dome, sometimes located at the crossing of a church.

Narthex: The arched porch or vestibule extending across a church's main entrance.

Nave: The main body of the church and bounded by the aisles. Contains the best seats in the house.

NORTHERN ITALY—MORE THAN JUST GREAT PASTA

Romanesque architecture probably originated in northern Italy in the late ninth century, but didn't reach its heyday until the mid-twelfth century. Ironically, the style never really won widespread acceptance in Rome.

One of the early trendsetting churches is the San Miniato al Monte in Florence (1018–1062). Although it's basically a basilica, the simple church features transverse arches that span the nave dividing it into discrete bays, serving as a prologue to the vaulted bays of later Gothic churches. Its novel exterior detailing with paneling and banding in black and white marble was used later in Gothic churches in Italy.

ONE CRAZY CAMPANILE

In Pisa stands—or I should say slants—one of the most famous buildings in the world. Every tacky tourist on a whirlwind Continental tour wants to visit the Leaning Tower of Pisa. (Only pretentious architect wannabees call this one a campanile, but, hey, you're reading this book so you can get to take your choice.) Yet it's only one structure of a trio of truly fine Romanesque buildings that unquestionably makes up one of the great architectural groupings of all time. Set on a grassy piazza, the Cathedral, Baptistery, and Campanile feature brilliant white marble exteriors and delicate ornamentation, which is out of character with mainstream Romanesque architecture.

The Cathedral is a double-aisled basilica, intersected by two smaller basilicas to form a transept with an elaborate dome over the crossing. The exterior features layers of arcades and pilasters. Right next door is the Baptistery, which came later (1153–1265) and is credited to Dioti Salvi. It features a circular plan with a central space measuring 60 feet in diameter.

But it's that eccentric Leaning Tower that gives Pisa its pizzazz. It rises thirteen stories to a height of 179 feet, and it now leans about 13 feet off center. The history books all say the celebrated slope is due to poor founda-

The perilous angle of the Campanile gets everyone's attention, but architecturally the Cathedral and Baptistery aren't exactly slouches.

tion work. (A few cynics claim that maybe it was intentional. Florence, Rome, and Venice are tough competition for tourism.) Regardless, the tower has fascinated civil engineers for almost a thousand years.

Granted Pisa buildings bend some of the rules of the Romanesque style (i.e., intense decoration and a relatively old-fashioned structural system), but this was an architecture that was in a constant flux and incorporated many influences. On the whole, Italian Romanesque shows much more interest in the creation of serene and spacious interiors than in technical adventure.

BYZANTINE CONTEMPORARIES: EAST MEETS WEST ALONG THE DITCHES OF VENICE

About the same time along the canals of Venice, things were developing with a decidedly different slant. In its early days, the merchant republic of Venice depended heavily on trade with Constantinople, and the economic intercourse carried over into its architecture. Venice's masterpiece of the period is St. Mark's. It is unlike any other church in the world because Venice is unlike any other city in the world.

The first church on the site was completed in 830 to house the remains of Evangelist, the patron saint of the sea. By 1063, the city made plans to replace the old church with another, grander structure (that was not completely finished for another five centuries). A rather gaudy repository for the spoils of war as well as a place of worship, St. Mark's shamelessly flaunts its loot, in-

(*continued*)

cluding the four golden horses obtained during the sacking of Constantinople in the thirteenth century.

St. Mark's features a cruciform plan with a gilded dome above each of the four arms and a taller dome crowning the central bay. The upper portion of the main facade is a fantasy of fifteenth-century gables, turrets, niches, and mosaics. The florid blend of Byzantine, Gothic, and Renaissance styles gives the church its almost fairy-tale appearance. Yet despite layers and layers of embellishments made between 1000 and 1690, the Byzantine core of St. Mark's looks much the way it did in the eleventh century.

Napoleon described the Piazza San Marco as the "greatest salon of Europe." It's still the finest spot in the world to sip espresso—and by the grace of God there's not a single Starbuck's in the whole bloody town.

THE FRENCH CONNECTION

The great era of French Romanesque architecture (1080–1150) was a time of political disjunction, and so the style there developed with an array of local influences. It's always been debated which region of France produces the best wine, and so it is with their architecture. Burgundy was the cradle of the great monastic orders of the Cluniacs and Cistercians. The Third Abbey Church at Cluny (1088–1130) with its massive walls, colossal nave, and countless towers was one of the grandest exemplars. It was a model for other churches for hundreds of years. Unfortunately, the church was demolished in 1810.

However, all were not lost. The beautiful Cluniac abbey church of St. Madeleine at Vezelay (1089–1206) was built as one of the great pilgrimage churches and it still welcomes tourists. Its interior is lighter and airier than most Romanesque churches and it features massive arches enlivened with pink and gray bands of stone.

But the region of Normandy stakes claim to the venerable French Romanesque church, St. Etienne in Caen (1068–1115). It was commissioned by William (in his spare time when he wasn't out conquering) as part of the Abbey-aux-Hommes. St. Etienne has a long nave in eight compartments and is entered from the west (like all good churches are positioned) through three portals. The long shafts in the nave were a foreshadowing of Gothic things to come. St. Etienne was typical of the great early Norman churches. (Norman is just the name given to Romanesque-style buildings constructed in the lands conquered by the Normans. So it's more a geographic designation than a stylistic variation.)

CHANNEL SURFING WITH A CERTAIN STYLE

In 1066, William decided to take his architectural ideas, as well as his powerful army, to the British Isles. The initial military campaign was quick and brutal, and the

Durham is Romanesque—not Gothic—and don't show your ignorance by confusing the two.

architectural conquest was equally effective. The Norman approach to design, like Norman rule, was ruthlessly logical. William oversaw building programs at Canterbury, Winchester, Rochester, and Worcester. St. Etienne served as a popular design model when they started erecting churches around the English countryside.

The most famous of the English churches of the style is the massive masonry Durham Cathedral. Perched atop an escarpment overlooking the River Ware, the Durham Cathedral is a masterpiece by any name. The plan is made up of a series of bays: eight in the nave, a square bay at the central crossing, and four bays to the east. It was the earliest European building to use ribbed vaults on a large scale—a key event in the evolution of Gothic architecture. Its half-barrel vaults over the gallery are, in effect, flying buttresses. Its massive circular piers have boldly incised patterns and vertical fluting. The visual logic and unity of each bay, complemented by the abstract patterns and spatial geometry, draw the eye up to the meeting point of the arches.

GERMANIC DOUBLE TAKES

Well-preserved Romanesque buildings are less common in Germany than in other parts of Europe. Blame some of the losses on World War II, but other churches just faded under the ravages of time. Limestone was scarce in most of Germany, so the material of choice was often sandstone, lava, or other less durable products. Some of the structures that haven't been lost have undergone sweeping remodelings. Five hundred years ago, restoration architects were oftentimes not very sympathetic to the original building and chose to leave their own mark and to reflect current tastes. Yet often under lots of added decoration, the original plan of the church remains.

German Romanesque churches are novel in planning and striking in scale. The must-sees on a German holiday include the cathedrals of Worms, Speyer, and Mainz. But St. Michael's at Hildesheim (1001–1033) was the most influential in shaping the layout of future churches. Rather than merely adding subsidiary chapels to the basic basilica, the builders of St. Michael's provided for two transepts, two apses, and two chancels arranged in an almost perfectly symmetrical plan.

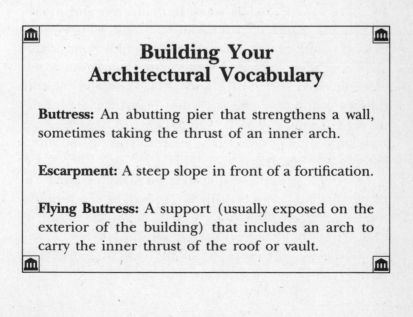

Building Your Architectural Vocabulary

Buttress: An abutting pier that strengthens a wall, sometimes taking the thrust of an inner arch.

Escarpment: A steep slope in front of a fortification.

Flying Buttress: A support (usually exposed on the exterior of the building) that includes an arch to carry the inner thrust of the roof or vault.

WHEN A ROMANESQUE CATHEDRAL SLIPS INTO BAROQUE CLOTHING

In the early days of the Dark Ages weird and miraculous powers were attributed to the holy relics of Jesus and his original twelve groupies, as well as most saints and martyrs. St. James, son of Zebedee, was interred in a modest tomb at Santiago de Compostela in northern Spain. By the middle of the ninth century, a Benedictine monastery had been established at Compostela. The Cathedral of St. James at Santiago de Compostela soon became the final destination on one of the most popular pilgrim routes on the Continent. Throngs of pious pedestrians risked life and limb to lay down their sorrows and soak up some powers from the highly charged remains. For the privilege, they were happy to couch up lots of gold and silver and probably some frankincense and myrrh. The monks gathered in the loot and built a huge cathedral—the undisputed masterpiece of Spanish Romanesque architecture, the Cathedral Santiago de Compostela. It was constructed between 1078 and 1211. Designed for continuous traffic flow, the cathedral features paired aisles flanking the massive barrel-vaulted nave. A massive octagonal lantern tower crowns the central crossing and filters lighting into the transepts below.

The original Romanesque exterior was "updated" in the eighteenth century with a flamboyant cloak of Baroque ornamentation, which we'll learn all about in Chapter 9. The slightly altered interior, however, still shows the weighty elegance of the structure itself and reflects the power of Romanesque austerity.

SUMMARY

 Romanesque architecture was reflective of the humble beginnings of a European culture, following the desolation of the Dark Ages.

 Christianity's original basilicas could no longer meet the needs of a popular religion. More preachers, pilgrims, and relics called for bigger and better buildings.

 The single great patron of the style was the Catholic Church.

 The Romanesque movement sprang up amidst a world of chaos, and the builders of the new style were constantly facing adversity, ranging from fire and war to overly demanding clients who thought they were God.

 It was a period of unceasing experimentation—a trial-and-error approach to design that took architecture, literally, to new heights.

 In spite of provincial peculiarities and idiosyncratic variations, there are consistencies. Decoration was never tacked on in a superficial way, but was derived from the actual structural supports of the building.

The style boasts lots of different faces, or facades, but basically it was a burly, brawny way of building borne out of a barbaric world.

CHAPTER 8

GOTHIC
(1140–1500)

YOU MUST REMEMBER THIS

Gothic might sound romantic to us today, but five hundred years ago it was the ultimate slur. Italian artists of the Renaissance (which came right on the heels of Gothic) considered the style so barbaric, they named it after the savage Goths who ravaged Rome in the fifth century. (It didn't seem to matter that the Goths had nothing to do with the development of their namesake style of architecture.) The basic components of Gothic architecture—the pointed arch, rib vault, flying buttress, and stained glass window—were not original in themselves but evolved during the preceding Romanesque period. What was innovative about the Gothic period was the fusion of these components in a revolutionary new structural and esthetic system with a dynamic unity. These were buildings much greater than the sum of their parts. Gothic architecture enjoyed almost universal popularity with the peoples of northern Europe and spread almost as fast as the bubonic plague.

MOST FAMOUS FOR

★ Abbey Church of St. Denis, outside Paris, France (1137–1144)
★ Nôtre Dame, Paris (1163–1250)
★ Chartres Cathedral, France (1194–1220)
★ Salisbury Cathedral, England (1220–1266)
★ Doges' Palace, Venice (1309–1424)

THE NEW STYLE THAT SELLS ITSELF

To understand an architectural style it's necessary to understand its individual features. But features alone do not make the style. There must be one central idea active in all of them. Many of the early Gothic motifs can be traced to Romanesque architecture. Their combination, however, was what was new and exciting. More importantly, this grandiose appearance met the physical and spiritual needs of the Church, as well as the aspirations of the people. This gave the style its higher purpose and meaning.

Gothic architecture evolved at a time of profound social and economic change on the Continent. In the late eleventh and twelfth centuries, trade and industry were revived. The isolationism of the feudal era gave way to the rise of new countries, many of which still exist in some form today.

Architectural styles spread more slowly in the days before global communications and jet-setting architects who developed their schematic designs on the flight from London to Tokyo. Considering the postmedieval scarcity of Federal Express, fax machines, or car phones, Gothic architecture spread surprisingly quickly throughout Europe.

THE UNDISPUTED LEADER
OF THE PACK

Few buildings in history were as revolutionary in their conception and so unhesitating in their execution as St. Denis Abbey outside of Paris. And we don't even know who was the architect. An ambitious abbot named Suger takes most of the credit for its construction. He also wrote two books about the abbey. Although its basic scheme is Romanesque and most elements had been seen before, the final effect is pure Gothic. The plan of the choir had two circular aisles with seven radiating chapels, each roofed by a ribbed vault with pointed arches. The heave buttresses that contain the outward pressure of the vaults can only be seen from the exterior. Time has not been kind to St. Denis; its main elevation and the upper section of the choir were rebuilt in the thirteenth century.

VARIETY IS THE SPICE OF LIFE

The Gothic cathedral was eminently adaptable. So much variation is possible in Gothic design that it is impossible to describe one building and call it typical. A church could be planned larger or smaller, longer or shorter, with or without transept, according to the desires of the congregation. It had no predetermined proportion of parts like the Greek temple or set plan like the Renaissance churches that would come later. The individuality of the Gothic cathedrals is quite extraordinary if one considers the mood of the world at the time. This was a period of rigid attitudes when conformity was the rule, improvisation was suspect, and departure from standard operating procedures could be construed as heresy.

ON THE BANKS OF THE SEINE

The festivities marking the dedication of St. Denis had barely concluded when the bishops of Sens, Reims,

Laon, Bourges, and Paris started planning cathedrals of their own. And you better believe that even twelfth-century Parisians weren't about to be outdone by a pack of country bumpkins. Begun in 1163, Nôtre Dame Cathedral in Paris was seminal in the evolution of the French Gothic style. At 110 feet tall, it is one of the first cathedrals built on a truly monumental scale. It features a compact cruciform plan with sexpartite vaulting (see Chapter 7) and colossal windows.

The Cathedral of Nôtre Dame in Paris stands tall, even if one of its most famous inhabitants had a slight hunch.

ONE BETTER IN CHARTRES

Medieval towns had few outlets for collective civic pride. The cathedral was about it, so intense rivalry led to higher and higher edifices. The Cathedral of Chartres certainly gave the locals something to shout about. The present cathedral was begun in 1194 after a devastating fire destroyed an earlier church and the bishop's palace

There might be more innovative structures, but Chartres Cathedral has an unsurpassed unity of conception and an amazing collection of windows. It's the supreme synthesis of Gothic art.

THE HUNDRED-YEAR MYTH
. . . .

**Gothic cathedrals are huge structures rich with orna-
mentation, but contrary to popular opinion, they didn't
always require centuries to build. Granted, the building
of some cathedrals did drag on, but the construction
time for many landmark churches was surprisingly
short. Apart from its belfries and some decorations that
were added much later, the Chartres Cathedral was
built in less than thirty years. The bulk of the Salisbury
Cathedral took just over forty years to build.**

---

next to it. The plan of Chartres is characterized by a
short nave and an atypically shaped choir, whose configuration was determined by the crypt of the older
church. The building's famous west facade is dominated
by two asymmetrical spires. The southern one was earlier
and shows an uncluttered restraint; the other one is a
marvel of High Gothic (a later version that appropriately
resulted in taller structures, as well as more ornamentation). The stained glass at Chartres is incredible—176
windows in all. More than 90 percent of the glass surface
is the original medieval glass.

THE ENGLISH WAY

Gothic architecture was introduced in England by the
French designer William of Sens, who had been invited
to rebuild the east end of Canterbury Cathedral after a
fire in 1174. By the time of the consecration of Canterbury ten years later, cathedrals in Wells and Lincoln were
under construction.

Things were developing differently in England. Gothic builders there emphasized length, not height or width. The French usually built their churches in the heart of downtown; the English preferred bucolic settings. Scores of English cathedrals survive. One of the great ones is Salisbury Cathedral, the only English Gothic church built in one generation as a single unit on a virgin site.

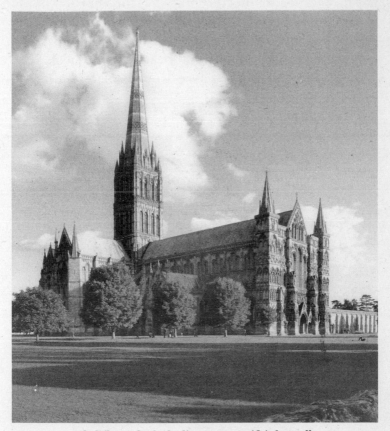

Salisbury Cathedral's tower at 404 feet tall was the loftiest spire of the Middle Ages.

LATE BLOOMER

Gothic came late to Italy, and it was never quite as popular there as it was in northern Europe. Gothic architecture came to be identified as something if not totally alien then certainly not native to Italy. However, between 1200 and 1400, Gothic was accepted in Italy because it was the style of architecture that had the approval of the Catholic Church.

Still, Italian Gothic is unlike the rest of Europe's, and most buildings there hardly deserve the label. The largest example of the style is the Milan Cathedral

Rumor has it that fifty architects worked on Milan Cathedral—no wonder the facade is so fussy.

(1386–1485). Its exterior is a mass of shimmering marble articulated with delicate pinnacles, ornate flying buttresses, and elaborate sculptures. Inside is dark and mysterious with massive molded piers and a vault rising to 148 feet.

As the Gothic style spread through Italy, it was adapted to secular structures like the Palazzo Vecchio (1298–1314) and the Ponte Vecchio (1345) in Florence. Its most outlandish manifestation of the style has got to be the Doges' Palace in Venice. The palace was started in the ninth century and rebuilt several times up until the Renaissance. Its exterior is an exuberant collage of pink-and-white patterned marble, a network of stacked arcades, ornate windows, and a lace-like parapet of oriental cresting.

The Florence Cathedral (1296–1462) started out as a Gothic church. But thanks to Filippo Brunelleschi (one of the true Renaissance men, see Chapter 9) who added a dome in 1434, it has come to be regarded as a mile-

Doges' Palace: It's a great piece of urban planning, but those funky facades make it unforgettable.

ISLAM ON THE IBERIAN PENINSULA

Islamic architecture in Spain and North Africa developed somewhat independently from most of the other lands that fell under rule of the Muslims. The Alhambra in Granada was built mainly in the fourteenth century as the palace and fortress of the last Islamic rulers of Spain, and it's one of their most richly decorated buildings of all time—a mystical affair of ceramic, stucco, plaster, delicate screens, and miniature columns. Lushly planted terraces, sparkling watercourses, and jewel-like pavilions abound. It's the only Islamic palace in Spain that survives basically intact.

stone of the incipient Renaissance. Don't be fooled, however. The beautiful green and white marble shell of the church is set atop a Gothic plan.

FALL FROM GRACE, AND THEN BACK UP FROM THE CRYPT

Gothic architecture fell out of fashion during the sixteenth century, and it would be three hundred years before the style was back in vogue with the Gothic Revival of the nineteenth century. Its proponents always believed the style had God on their side. In 1836 a British architect named A.W.N. Pugin wrote that Gothic was both "morally and esthetically the only correct and universal style."

Scores of famous cathedrals and churches were built in Europe and in the United States during the style's

*The British Houses of Parliament (1840–1865), dominating
the skyline of Westminster, established Gothic as a style befitting
public monuments as well as religious edifices.*

revival, but this time cast-iron beams and girders were
concealed behind the stonework for that extra support.
New York City's Trinity Church (1839–1846), designed
by Richard Upjohn, is one of the best known neo-Gothic
churches in the United States. Some congregations even
decided to revive the original way of building. In Washington, D.C., the Cathedral of St. Peter and St. Paul (or

more commonly called the National Cathedral) was built stone on stone in the traditional Gothic manner without benefit of a hidden steel structural system.

SUMMARY

⏱ Gothic architecture achieved technical advances, but these innovations were solely a means to an end. The spiritual symbolism of the style was its main selling point and the driving force behind its rapid adoption.

⏱ Architects of the day designed a few castles, forts, and civic buildings, but the Church hogged most of the design talent. It was in the service of the Church that the Gothic style reached its apex (not to put too fine a point on it).

⏱ Gothic architecture has no fixed set of proportions, such as the height-to-diameter ratio of a Classical column, so there is great variation in a period famous for rigid attitudes about most aspects of life.

⏱ Gothic architecture was the final expression of the medieval world—the physical manifestation of the concepts of a mystical cosmos and a transcendental religion.

⏱ Gothic architecture was not a stepping stone for another style that was to follow. It didn't evolve into another style; it was an esthetic unique unto itself.

CHAPTER 9

RENAISSANCE AND BAROQUE
(1400–1700)

YOU MUST REMEMBER THIS

Renaissance means quite simply "rebirth," but it was a selective resuscitation—only the Classical models of Greece and Rome were deemed worthy of revival. It was the first major instance of self-appointed creative types self-consciously plundering the past for inspiration. They obviously thought it was better to be good than original. Their rediscovery of antiquity's ideals, as well as its columns, pilasters, pediments, and temples, transformed the appearance of architecture, starting in Florence and moving throughout Europe. Buildings became esthetic phenomena and architects metamorphosed into artists rather than mere craftsmen. Renaissance architecture evolved into Baroque and later Neoclassicism with the Classical spirit holding its own until the turn of the twentieth century.

MOST FAMOUS FOR

★ Foundling Hospital, Florence, Italy (1419–1424)
★ St. Peter's, Rome, Italy (1506–1667)
★ Villa Rotonda, near Vicenza, Italy (1550–1554)
★ Escorial, near Madrid, Spain (1562–1582)
★ Château de Chambord, France (1519–1547)
★ St. Paul's Cathedral, London, England (1675–1710)

A STYLE IS BORN—AND AT A HOME FOR UNWED MOTHERS, NO LESS

A hot new style of architecture won't go very far without clients who have money to build the actual buildings. Not to worry. In Italy a unique new social hierarchy was emerging—a merchant class with unprecedented wealth and power. Even back then, a surefire way for the nouveau riche to buy respectability was to focus on a charity, donate major money to the cause, then hire a big-name architect to design a building.

By the early 1400s, the Medicis were one such rising clan vying for social and political clout in Florence. In 1419, Giovanni de'Medici hired Filippo Brunelleschi to design the Foundling Hospital. (It was actually an orphanage, but that's an outdated term. Today's euphemism would probably be something nondescript, like the Home for Children.)

A design masterpiece by any name, the Foundling Hospital is by most accounts the first pure Renaissance building. Brunelleschi used details—arches, columns, and Corinthian capitals—that echoed antiquity. However, the loggia (that's the space created by the arcade, or simply a porch) with its very slender columns and delicate semicircular arches looked decidedly different from the chunkier structures of ancient Rome. Even before it was completed, the building was the subject of discussion, and news of its unique appearance spread.

It was a rousing success on many levels. Brunelleschi became a star, and the Medicis won the support of the city's downtrodden, as well as its intelligentsia. However, that there should be a benevolent function for the Renaissance's inaugural building would prove to be the exception rather than the rule. More typical of the Renaissance were fortress-like courtyard homes, such as the Palazzo Medici-Riccardi and the Palazzo Rucellai, designed for significantly richer residents.

WHO'S WHO ☞

Real Renaissance Men Don't Eat Quiche

Filippo Brunelleschi (1377–1446).
Trained as a sculptor and goldsmith. Classical scholar in his spare time. Nixed on getting the big job—to design new bronze doors for the Florence Baptistery—he turned to architecture. Responsible for Florence Cathedral dome (see Chapter 8) and for Foundling Hospital. One of many who dabbled at St. Peter's.

Leon Battista Alberti (1404–1472).
A dogmatic theorist whose writings were as influential, if not more so, as his buildings. The Palazzo Rucellai and the St. Maria Novella were his best efforts.

Donato Bramante (1444–1514).
Introduced the Renaissance to Rome with a nifty little building called the Tempietto, a circular chapel only 15 feet in diameter and surrounded by a Tuscan colonnade and crowned by a dome. Won the initial competition to design St. Peters, but was replaced by a litter of

WHO'S WHO

(continued)

lesser architects who accomplished very little there until Michelangelo burst onto the scene.

Michelangelo Buonarroti (1475–1564).
Didn't take up architecture until late middle age, but he amassed an incredible collection of buildings for an old man who spent the best years of his life flat on his back painting the Sistine Chapel. At age 72, he revived Bramante's original St. Peter's idea for Greek-cross plan and added the dome.

Giovanni Lorenzo Bernini (1598–1680).
Lead Italy into the Baroque period. In 1629, he took over at the Vatican (as architect, not pope) and designed the embracing elliptical piazza in front of St. Peter's.

A SYSTEM IS BORN—IN THE DRAWING ROOM OF THE RICHEST GUY IN TOWN

Private patronage was now the driving force behind building. Civic and religious functions often took a back seat to the egos of individuals. Architecture became almost a private matter between patron and architect— and their buildings were to be monuments to both. The

Renaissance drew heavily on existing Classical models for inspiration, yet the architects of the day who were coping the buildings of antiquity got much more respect than any of the original designers in Rome and Greece. Architects were no longer just masons, builders, or craftsmen; they were full-fledged artists with celebrity status. As a result, they got invited to all the best parties. But now they had to network constantly to get their next job.

The patronage system was elitist, but it encouraged individualism as at no previous time in history. Classicism was the only way to go, but there was a lot of room for mixing and matching Greek and Roman doodads—columns, pediments, arches, domes, friezes, etc. The landmark buildings of the Renaissance were highly personal creations, the result of a collaboration between a patron who knew what he wanted and an architect who could deliver the esthetic goods.

Architects were now ensconced on their own stylistic pedestals. Not much has changed in the past five hundred years, and many architects have come to rue their precariously prominent positions, subject always to prevailing winds.

DIVINE INTERVENTION—OR PIOUS POMP AND CIRCUMSTANCE

By the end of the fifteenth century, Rome was usurping Florence as the Renaissance powerhouse. In 1503, Julius II became Pope and launched a massive urban renewal program drawing from a list of architects comprising a virtual Who's Who of the Renaissance (see sidebar). By

St. Peter's is one of those great buildings that manages to tell everybody who's in charge, when nobody really needs reminding.

the seventeenth century, thanks to Michelangelo's dome and Bernini's network of colonnades, fountains, and foreground piazza, the Vatican featured a splendor befitting the center of Christendom. However, St. Peter's isn't perfect. It lacks a true architectural unity (but what do you expect when dozens of egotistical popes and architects are involved), and head-on exterior views of the dome are obscured by the extreme length and height of the nave.

PUBLISH AND PROCREATE

Although he didn't work on the scale or have the great sites of the other big Renaissance honchos, Andrea Palladio (1508–1580) is probably the most influential or at least the most-copied architect of all time. He is that rare bird who gave his name to a popular style of architecture—Palladianism—not to mention those ubiquitous arched Palladian windows that transform a tacky suburban house into an expensive tacky suburban house.

His claim to fame is a bunch of houses for some farmers in the Veneto region of northern Italy. Palladio was a genius when it came to getting the most design to the ducat (or bang for the buck). He developed a stripped-down architecture, which relied for its effect not on fine materials or careful detailing but on proportion and composition. The walls were plastered brick, with no attempt to imitate stone. The building was rendered flat and given a coat of paint. This style was not only cheaper to build but cheaper to design; good business, too, because then as now reduced budgets meant reduced architectural fees.

His masterpiece is the Villa Rotonda, also called the Villa Capra (1565–1569), set on a commanding hill outside Vicenza and built as a country retreat rather than as a working farm. The symmetrical plan has a circular hall crowned with a low central dome (hence the name "Rotonda"). Basically, he developed every real estate agent's dream combination—a sense of Classical sophistication with that comfortable "lived-in" look.

Most of Palladio's country villas, of which some twenty examples survive, were built as planned. Credit goes to the landed gentry who hired Palladio. The Villa Emo is still inhabited by descendants of the original clients.

Palladio was above all a domestic architect, the first whose career and reputation were founded not on religious or even civic buildings but on houses for the rich and famous. But everybody who was anybody had to do at least a couple of churches, and Palladio was no exception. His two great Venetian churches, San Giorgio Maggiore and II Redentore, show his equally masterful adaptation of Classical forms for habitation by a Higher Power.

What really cemented Palladio's reputation was his publication of a number of unabashedly self-promoting books, entitled the *Four Books of Architecture*—the kind of slick presentation you might see from a large architecture firm today. He was also the first architect whose international reputation was based not on firsthand experience of his buildings, most of which were in remote locations, but on widespread popularity of his books. Palladio would later be rediscovered by the English architect Inigo Jones (see page 134) around the turn of the seventeenth century. The books were reissued and they sold like hot scones in Great Britain, providing the model for the grand English and American country houses of the eighteenth century.

THEY DON'T BUILD PIAZZAS LIKE THEY USED TO

The Piazza Navona epitomizes the Baroque in Rome. Borromini designed the Sant'Agnese Church, Bernini designed the two glorious fountains, and Pietro da Cortona (1596–1669) painted the gallery in the Pamphili Palace.

THE SPREAD OF THE RENAISSANCE

North of the Alps, the influx of the principles and forms of Classicism was haphazard and belated. At first the Renaissance building style took the form of small features and superficial decoration on what were basically Gothic structures. This uneasy juxtaposition of local building techniques and imported Italian ideas first appeared in the Loire valley of France.

By the fifteenth century, France was emerging as a strong monarchy with a large aristocracy. The French have never been known for their restraint, and their earliest buildings are no exception. A major player in the French Renaissance was Francois I. He built the vast Château of Chambord (1519–1547) as a palatial hunting lodge when it was still PC to shoot small animals and birds. Its immense round towers and bizarre turreted skyline are medieval, but its main block, or donjon, is

BAROQUE: ANOTHER STYLISTIC SLUR

The term "baroque" originally meant a misshapen or rough pearl. Granted the style can be ostentatious and pretentious and maybe even gaudy, but the archaic interpretation of the term is hardly applicable to the enticing vitality of this late Renaissance period. Architecture was much more dramatic and structurally daring than ever before. Designers embraced the flowing aspects of sculpture and incorporated the high-contrast effects of painting. Undulating facades, serpentine volumes, complex oval interior plans, and marble, gilt, and bronze abounded.

Unsubstantiated rumors that Leonardo da Vinci was partially responsible for the design of Chambord are probably just that.

Italianate in plan. The exterior facades are a virtual farrago (that's Latin for "hodgepodge") of niches, columns, pilasters, and dormers.

In the city of Paris, Francois I initiated the rebuilding of a medieval mansion—another well-known French landmark, the Palace of the Louvre in 1546. It wasn't completed until 1875 (or 1989 if you count I. M. Pei's pyramid in the courtyard). The Louvre is a textbook representation in stone of the evolution of French Renaissance architecture. Pierre Lescot's original redesign of the section of the building known as Cour Carree (Court of Carree) uses the Italian language, but with a decidedly French accent. The Louvre was built upon over hundreds of years, and in the end, it has proven to be an adaptable building.

*The Baroque style came to France in a big way at Versailles
(1661–1756). It was the embodiment of Louis XIV's
absolutism in design as well as politics, not to mention
his wanton self-indulgence. Money was obviously no object.*

IT WAS THE BEST OF ROOFS; IT WAS THE WORST OF ROOFS

François Mansart (1598–1666) was the greatest French architect of his day. But he was obstinate and boorish in his dealings with clients, which cost him many an aristocratic commission. When he didn't blow the job, he created buildings that are models of restraint and clarity, such as the Orleans Wing at Blois, the Maisons-Lafitte, and the Val de Grace. Mansart also gave his name to the mansard roof—a design that features a flat upper part with steeply pitched sides. It didn't seem to matter that Mansart neither invented the form nor used it very often. The mansard roof is one of those good ideas (like Nobel's dynamite) that somehow turns into a disaster in the wrong hands. The roofline is a major component in a short-lived style called Second Empire, named after a short-lived French Empire. (Philadelphia City Hall and the Old Executive Office Building in Washington, D.C., are the American versions.)

Northern Exposure

The architects of Germany, Austria, Belgium, and Holland relied less on strict Classical precedents than did their contemporary practitioners in Italy and France. They hung onto Gothic ideas, as well as nonacademic approaches to design. Ironically, much of central Eu-

WHEN ARCHITECTS MOONLIGHT

rope's early Renaissance architecture was overstated, while by the time the Baroque rolled in, their designs were relatively restrained.

One of the first northern European buildings in the true Renaissance spirit is the town Hall in Antwerp (1561–1565). Designed by Cornelis Floris, the Town Hall is a confident and idiosyncratic use of the Classical orders and served for generations as a model for other town halls in the Low Countries. Its dynamic four-story front facade has an imposing central frontispiece with half columns in a continuous triumphal arch motif.

Architects of the Low Countries continued to develop their own design elaborations, in terms of both ornament and form of the front facades. The Guild Houses on the Grande Place of old Brussels were built in the 1690s. Their sculptural vibrancy and overdone ornamentation are Classical in its loosest definition, but Belgian to the bone.

ROCOCO: WAS IT REALLY BAD OR DID IT JUST SUFFER FROM BAD PR?

Originating in Paris, Rococo was characterized by exquisite, light-hearted decorations and interiors with an affinity for pastel colors. Motifs included flowers, shells, scrolls, and clouds in refined compositions. Rococo was delicate and eschewed the structural bravado of Baroque. But Rococo's undoing was its popularity among the aristocracy. When the resplendent style came to be identified with a decadent upper class, Rococo fell out of favor relatively abruptly around the end of the eighteenth century. And then, there were the Modernists who thought the style was the nadir of architecture.

CENTRAL EUROPEAN
DEVELOPMENTS

Renaissance architecture came slowly and sporadically to Germany, and opened to mixed reviews. Heidelberg Castle, which was developed and expanded from 1531 to 1615, is uncharacteristically garish for its time and place. Critics have called the ornate facades of the Friedrichsbau section of the castle less a building than a field for decoration.

The Thirty Year's War (1618–1648), a major conflict between northern European Protestants and the powerful Hapsburg Empire, took its toll on Bavaria, Austria, and Bohemia. But by the beginning of the eighteenth century this region was building some pretty impressive religious, residential, and secular structures. First Baroque and then Rococo took root in Bavaria.

But again, the Church was really the big player in the world of architecture. Martin Luther, and his pesky little Protestant Reformation, was giving the Catholic establishment some competition. A wave of religious fervor led to a building program by the Catholic Church to keep the pious placated. The Benedictine Monastery of Melk (1702–1714) was given a more dramatic presence when it was rebuilt using the designs of Jakob Prandtauer. The grand monastery stands on a commanding bluff overlooking the Danube; a domed church anchors the compound.

Court architect Johann Bernhard Fischer von Erlach (1656–1723) was busy building three churches (with *really* long names) in Salzburg. But the church of his to remember is the eclectic Karlskirche in Vienna, started in 1716 and completed fourteen years after his death. The plan is a fusion of an oval and a Greek cross, while the facade is almost twice as wide as the actual building that it screens. However, its most novel feature are two columns modeled on those of Trajan and Marcus Aurelius in Rome. He also crossed the border to design the Abbey Church at Ottobeuren (1749–1767), one of the grandest and largest German Rococo churches. It's a sumptuous concoction of marble, frescoes, colorful stucco walls, and gold stucco frames, but it features spatial simplicity with a clean plan.

A Grim Reminder of a Grim Regime

Few royal compounds were better suited to its original resident than the Escorial, home to Philip II of Spain.

The Escorial, with its severe exterior, implied asceticism, and massive scale, has been called a magnificent aberration as well as the most forbidding structure in Christendom.

He came to the throne in 1556 and ruled for the rest of the century. Philip II believed that the forcible establishment of Catholicism—in other words, the Spanish Inquisition—was the best way to achieve political unity and create an empire over which he and the Pope would preside. Philip was destined to fail (remember England's defeat of the Spanish Armada in 1588?), but in the meantime he built a building like nothing else before or since.

The Escorial (1559–1582) is an austere grouping of buildings set on a lonely mountain site outside Madrid. It's a royal court, monastery, college, church, and home to a real holy tyrant. Juan Bautista de Toledo was the original architect, and Juan de Herrera completed the

A WINDOW TO THE WEST— AND WHAT ABOUT THE CURTAINS!

In 1703, Peter the Great founded the new city of St. Petersburg. It was the first modern capital built to a predetermined plan; Rome, Paris, and Stockholm provided the inspiration. But it was when the women in the family were in charge that the city really bloomed. Elizabeth, who ruled from 1741 to 1762, with her official architect Bartolomeo Rastrelli, built churches, the Smolny Convent, and of course, several royal houses. The most famous is the Winter Palace, a gigantic, fifty-bay extravaganza painted turquoise-blue and white that presents a dramatic sculptural backdrop for the Palace Square. Catherine the Great, who was in charge from 1762 to 1796, continued the royal building process with such landmarks as the Hermitage Theater and the Academy of Fine Arts in St. Petersburg.

scheme. The entire complex is built of granite. The ground plan is in the shape of a grid with fifteen courtyards set on either side of a central axis. The august majesty of its composition extends to the smallest detail—totally consistent with Philip's maniacally obsessive approach to living and governing.

No Architect Is an Island

England is separated from the Continent by a relatively narrow channel of water, yet this gulf has always been wide enough to give the British Isles a cultural and artistic detachment.

Architecture developments from 1500 to 1830 didn't fall into the neat classifications that characterize the rest of the Renaissance. England developed its own labels for its own unique minimovements that never really took off anywhere else. Tudor was a late-English Gothic architecture featuring low timber roofs and exposed wooden rafters that became a major part of the decoration. Tudor evolved into Elizabethan, which incorporated large-scale, watered-down Renaissance motifs. Jacobean was the name given to a more unified early Renaissance architecture, whose common characteristics included brick with stone dressings, capped turrets, and Flemish gables.

Although the Renaissance hit Italy in the fifteenth century, the movement barely touched England before the seventeenth century. When it finally arrived in full force, England responded with an architecture that was much more conservative than what was going up in the rest of

Europe. British architects seldom matched the monumentality of Italians, the expressive fervor of Germans, or the poetic romanticism of French, but they are hard to beat when it comes to dignity and practicality.

KEEPING UP WITH THE JONESES

One architect almost single-handedly brought the Renaissance to merry olde England. His name was Inigo Jones (1573–1652). He was the first Brit to study in earnest the Roman antiquities and to assimilate the Classical precepts of Vitruvius (see Chapter 4) and Palladio. Jones pushed the traditions of Classicism—pure geometrical shapes, interrelated proportions, and the "correct" forms and symbolic language of the orders. Few of his buildings survive, but the ones that do reveal his radical, albeit rehashed, approach to architecture. His first major commission was the Queen's House (1616–1618) in Greenwich, and it represented the first English villa built in the Italian style. Next came his Banqueting House in the Whitehall section of London, which was completed in 1622 and was strictly Palladian in concept. It's a building of Classical perfection, balancing stasis and movement in an entirely Renaissance manner to form a harmonious composition.

Jones basically restricted his work to royal circles and his "stiff-upper-lip" style of design was adopted in full only by his apprentice John Webb, who incidentally married Jones's niece. Webb designed the King Charles Block at Greenwich Palace, but he never matched his master in terms of artistic creativity or subtle sophistication.

SEIZE THE DAY

Sir Christopher Wren (1632–1723) is to English architecture what Shakespeare is to English literature. He was
28 years old in 1660, when Charles II was restored to
the throne, and a year later he found himself with the
job of assistant to the royal surveyor. It didn't seem to
matter that he was primarily a mathematician, astronomer, and classical scholar. Wren's great opportunity
arose after London's Great Fire of 1666, which raged for
days, destroying eighty-eight churches including the old
St. Paul's, and 13,000 houses and shops along hundreds
of blocks of prime downtown real estate. Wren didn't
waste any time. Within nine days he delivered a plan to
Charles II for the rebuilding of the city—a formal
scheme with a series of squares and radiating streets at
the center of which was to be a new St. Paul's Cathedral.

Without the backing of a pope or an absolute monarch, Wren had some initial trouble getting the project
off the ground. The people of London disdained foreign
styles of design, which they associated with the excesses
of the monarchy, and the Church of England scorned
anything that smacked of Roman Catholicism. Wren had
his work cut out for him. He had to scrap his original
scheme for a centralized church in the tradition of Bramante and Michelangelo, as well as his backup idea for
a church with curved walls. At last, everybody agreed on
a Latin-cross plan with a wide nave and a low dome.

St. Paul's cornerstone was laid in 1675, and Wren was
given the authority to make changes during construction. It was completed in 1710, spanning practically
Wren's entire career and showing his synthesis of Classi-

cal Renaissance forms and Baroque detailing. The dome grew, and it's an engineering marvel, with a brick cone set between the inner round cupola and the outer pointed shell.

Wren lived to the ripe old age of 91, and he never let up. He designed more than fifty other churches, including the neo-Gothic St. Dunstan-in-the-East, and his more Baroque St. Bride on Fleet Street. His campus buildings include the Pembroke and Trinity College chapels at Cambridge and the Sheldonian Theatre at Oxford.

St. Paul's rivals Rome's St. Peter's, and it's considered England's only truly Classical cathedral.

**WHO SAID IT? GIVE CREDIT
WHERE CREDIT IS DUE**
. . . .
The famous triad of "utilitas, firmitas, and venustas"
was written by the roman architect Vitruvius. However,
Sir Henry Wotton, an early-seventeenth century British
diplomat, said it first in English. Wotton, most remem-
bered for his fishing skills as a "compleat angler," was
the subject of a biography by his friend Izaak Walton.
But Wotton was also an amateur architecture buff and
wrote a book called *The Element of Architecture,* which
begins: "Well building has three conditions; Commodity,
Firmness, and Delight."

THROWING A CURVE

Classical ideas were also applied to whole towns. Good
ol' Vitruvius had espoused some pretty radical ideas for
urban planning. His theoretical octagonal town plan features a central piazza and eight radial roads that offered
grand vistas. In addition, the town was designed to be
easily fortified. A Frenchman named Pierre L'Enfant
took cues from Vitruvius when he designed the plan for
Washington, D.C., in 1791.

Due to the rash of building in cities, savvy British architects started diversifying their practices to take a more
active role in town planning. One of the most spectacular examples was the work of a father-and-son team
(John Wood and John Wood II), who turned the small
English town of Bath into the most fashionable spa of
the day for wealthy hypochondriacs. Inspired by the

models of ancient Rome and Greece, they built the Queen's Square (1729–1736), Circus (1754), and finally the Royal Crescent (1767–1775). A giant half moon of a building detailed with a grand order of Ionic columns, the Royal Crescent is made up of thirty terraced houses that look like one continuous palatial facade. The arrangement carves out a pleasure park of open space and landscaping.

ALL GOOD THINGS
MUST COME TO PASS

In the end, the architecture of the Renaissance became the architecture of self-glorification of the popes, kings, and aristocrats. The ideal of beauty was a major influence on Renaissance art and architecture, but as time passed this larger objective was lost in the decoration. Baroque grew in embellishments and Rococo verged on mere prettiness, but social issues rather than esthetics were the real undoing of these styles.

Architectural theorists of the late-eighteenth century got caught up in the same dynamics that captivated the philosophers of the day. Buildings, it was deemed, should express the more essential elements of society. Architect Claude Nicholas Ledoux (1736–1806), who was the Rousseau or maybe the Voltaire of design, did a lot of talking. He also designed a few fine and innovative buildings, especially in terms of their uses. Social awareness was increasing, and spawning new building types such as asylums, orphanages, prisons, schools, model factories, and worker housing.

The Royal Crescent created a romantic vocabulary for planning that was repeated throughout England.

The rising middle class started to believe they deserved more power and status. An architecture associated with the lifestyles of a decadent ruling class came to be detested and discarded. The people were ready for change.

SUMMARY

⏱ Renaissance architecture was a full-fledged resumption of the Classical system of proportions and elements (columns, pilasters, pediments, entablatures), but without relying on the simple structural principles of Greek design or the massiveness of Roman architecture.

⏱ Ornament was used only when it wouldn't detract from the precision of the individual parts or the clarity of the whole composition.

⏱ The buildings of the Renaissance were a personal collaboration between patron and designer.

⏱ In the Renaissance, architects became respected artists and started mingling with the upper crust of society.

⏱ Renaissance architecture evolved into Baroque, a much more sculptural, fluent, plastic, and artistic approach to design. Paintings and sculptures were integral to Baroque building.

CHAPTER 10

NINETEENTH CENTURY

YOU MUST REMEMBER THIS

Political insurrections were widespread, bringing vast social and economic changes. The major influence on architecture was the Industrial Revolution, which had started in Great Britain in the last quarter of the eighteenth century and gradually expanded across Europe and into the New World. Progressive structures of the period were marvels of engineering, using materials like iron, plate glass, and reinforced concrete in new types of construction.

But innovation can be threatening, and the nineteenth century was dominated by a revival of literal Classicism and historical themes. Architecture was more than mere fashion, and these styles provided powerful associative qualities: Roman stood for justice; Greek, for government and banking; Gothic, for religion and education; and Italianate for commerce.

MOST FAMOUS FOR

★ University of Virginia, Charlottesville, Virginia (1817–1826), Thomas Jefferson
★ British Museum, London (1823–1846), R. Smirke
★ Crystal Palace, London (1851), Joseph Paxton
★ Paris Opera (1861–1875), Charles Garnier
★ Trinity Church, Boston (1872–1877), Henry Hobson Richardson

REACHING FOR THE NEW, NOT LETTING GO OF THE OLD

The nineteenth century was the big transition period between the decline of the Renaissance and the rise of the foundations of Modernism. (We'll take a few liberties and extend beyond a strict interpretation of the calendar, the way "the 1960s" are more than simply a ten-year period.) The revolutions of the late 1700s and early 1800s wreaked havoc on the royal establishments. In terms of architecture, the political revolts inspired no new styles. Instead, the disorder brought still another Classical revival and a recapitulation of Romanesque, Gothic, Renaissance, Baroque, and exotic designs.

From the capitals of Europe to small towns in America, economic and political power had now passed, for the most part, into the hands of a new capitalist middle class. These bourgeois patrons were not encumbered with a rich tradition of good taste. They flaunted their new wealth and civic pride in a horde of neo-whatever styles. If religion is the opiate of the masses as Karl Marx maintained, then historicist architecture is the equivalent of an ice-cold beer.

DESIGNS FOR A NEW DEMOCRACY

When it came time to choose a suitable style of architecture for the new American Republic, the founding fathers turned to the old-fashioned models of ancient Greece and Rome. A major player was Thomas Jefferson (1743–1826), who kept busy designing when he wasn't writing the Declaration of Independence and running the country.

As minister to France, Jefferson visited the Maison Carree at Nimes (see Chapter 4) and was bowled over by its elegant Classical proportions and details. It was his model for the State Capitol (1789–1798) in Richmond, Virginia, that in turn served as the inspiration for hundreds of civic buildings throughout the fledging nation. His own house, Monticello (1796–1808), is a unique interpretation of a Palladian villa. He combined red brick, marble, and wood, and adapted a traditional floor plan to one of his own, to build a house perfectly suited to his lifestyle and its bucolic mountaintop setting.

ARCHITECTURE, BY GEORGE

Those egotistical British monarchs. Not only did they want to rule the world, they wanted their own namesake architecture. Queen Anne and the four Georges, who governed from 1702 to 1830, came up with the catchy title of "Georgian." The heyday of the style roughly aligned with their reigns. In addition to a natural popularity in the British Isles, Georgian architecture was the dominate style in the thirteen original colonies from 1700 to 1780. Its eighty-year reign makes it one of the longest lived styles of American architecture.

Georgian buildings are usually simple one- or two-story boxes with doors and windows arranged in strict symmetry. The style is characterized by a center paneled front door with intricate moldings and usually crowned with an elaborate top, like an entablature supported by ornate pilasters. Windows are double-hung sashes with small panes; most roofs are side gabled.

By Jefferson's own admission, one of his proudest accomplishments was the design of the University of Virginia in Charlottesville (1817–1826). He was aided by William Thornton (original architect of the U.S. Capitol) and Benjamin H. Latrobe (architect of the Catholic Cathedral in Baltimore, Maryland). The plan consists of a wide, rectangular open space, "the lawn," bordered on each of its longer sides by five double-story teaching pavilions with Classical porticoes and a continuous low colonnade connecting the student dorm rooms.

Jefferson's "academical village" at Charlottesville set a model for campus planning in the United States. Harvard might be older, but U.Va. has the best-laid plan.

A VERY ENGLISH APPROACH

When the Brits weren't building in their favorite neo-Gothic style (see Chapter 8), they found time to construct a lot of Neoclassical designs. The new Neoclassicism did not appear overnight; it required a rather long incubation with a few false starts. Some scholars even have trouble distinguishing between regular old Classicism and Neoclassicism, so don't feel bad if you can't either. Sir John Soane (1752–1837), a slightly neurotic but obviously talented designer, was on the cutting edge of the new approach in Britain. His masterpiece was the Bank of England (1788–1823), adapted from a round Roman temple. Soane left visible the cast-iron frame that supported the glasswork—a revolutionary concept at the time. The cavernous interior halls recall the grand interiors of ancient Rome. (Don't go looking for the original; it was mostly demolished except for a couple of facades. It was rebuilt in the 1930s.)

A fine late example of the style is the British Museum (1823–1846), designed by Sir Robert Smirke. It's a Greek Revival scheme with an imposing lineup of forty-eight Ionic columns along the south front and a pediment articulated with projecting sculpture.

PARISIAN MAKEOVER

In France, civic designs reflected a similar Neoclassical monumentality, but the model was usually Rome's resplendence rather than Greece's harmony. Vignon's Church of the Madeleine (1806–1842) is an almost literal reproduction of a Roman temple.

But looking beyond an isolated building here or there, it was Napoleon III's large-scale urban renewal that really changed the face of Paris in the nineteenth century.

George Haussmann laid out a series of wide boulevards
that transformed the old medieval urban core into a
grand Baroque city. His scheme was far more than an
esthetic gesture. In the aftermath of revolutionary street
fighting, controlling mobs was a major consideration. Between 1853 and 1870, his radiating plan with broad avenues cut a swathe through neighborhoods that might
have provided cover for political agitators. These new
avenues were lined with new five- and six-story apartment
buildings. Regardless of the imperialistic leanings of
Haussmann and Napoleon III, thanks to that dynamic
duo Paris remains one of the most beautiful cities in
the world.

Meanwhile, architect Charles Garnier was working on

The Paris Opera has been likened to an overloaded
sideboard, but the Phantom still calls it home.

the building that would come to epitomize the excesses of Napoleon III's empire—the Paris Opera House. The style is monumental neo-Baroque. Inside and out, the building is a triumph of sumptuous decoration with multicolored marbles, onyxes, and lavish gilded sculptures.

SPRINGTIME FOR UNIFIED DESIGNS IN GERMANY

Architects in Berlin in the nineteenth century also looked for inspiration from the past to produce buildings that would represent their patrons as upstanding role models who possessed enlightened values. The prolific German architect Karl Friedrich Schinkel (1748–1841) especially understood the power of architecture to set the right mood. One of his major buildings is the Schauspielhaus (1819–1821) in Berlin, a powerful Greek Revival design with bold massing. A few years later, he designed the Altes Museum, also in Berlin. Its facade features an intimidating screen of marching Ionic columns. The attic hides an enormous two-story domed rotunda.

FANTASIES REALIZED

The single-mindedness and clarity of style characterized by the Greek Revival of the mid-1800s was to be short-lived. As the century progressed, eclectic designs became all the rage, and the picturesque and exotic became increasingly common. British architect John Nash (1752–1835) started out as a Neoclassicist, but wasn't bashful about indulging in a sort of architectural costume ball when the spirit moved him. His eccentric masterpiece is the Royal Pavilion at Brighton, an unrestrained concoction of Moorish, Hindu, Chinese, and Gothic elements. But don't judge a fantasy by its facade. Underneath all those minarets, onion domes, and pinnacles is an innovative cast-iron structural system—one of the first instances of its use in a residence.

THE REAL MAGIC KINGDOM

Mad Ludwig II of Bavaria loved ostentatious architecture and he built three palaces that prove it: Schloss Linderhof, a late Rococo extravaganza (1874–1878); Herrenchiemsee, an island chateau based on Versailles (1878); and his most famous—a medieval fairy-tale castle called Neuschwanstein (1869–1881), designed by Eduard Riedel. In the spirit of a Wagnerian opus (Richard Wagner was Ludwig's buddy), Neuschwanstein

Ludwig II's fairy-tale castle dream come true.

(continued)

erupts from its rocky mountain site with turrets, towers, and terrific decorations. The castle was way too outlandish to influence real architects, and by the time of its completion, monarchs who valued their heads understood that such buildings could send the wrong message to their subjects. However, one savvy American entrepreneur thought the image was just perfect for his kingdom and chose it for the centerpiece of a little amusement park he was building in Anaheim, California.

Walt Disney's fairy-tale capitalist dream come true.

SAY YOU WANT A REVOLUTION

While much nineteenth-century architecture was grossly sentimental, the Industrial Revolution brought real changes in the development of new building materials and construction techniques. Structural systems that had existed only in theory became reality. Yet many architects of the day viewed the Industrial Revolution as a dangerous movement that threatened civilization as they knew it.

The most innovative buildings were oftentimes the fruits of engineers. They exploited the new materials of iron and glass to create simple, dignified buildings, such as dockyards, factories, viaducts, textile mills, and most memorably the great railway stations. Throughout the English countryside, these refreshingly functional structures still stand—many in regions endowed with few grand designs—holdovers from the blossoming machine age. Mechanical systems like central heating, running water and plumbing, electric lighting, and electric elevators were gradually incorporated in civic, commercial, and apartment buildings, yet the outer

---

VICTORIAN ARCHITECTURE
Queen Victoria ruled Britain from 1840 to 1901. The era is famous for its uptight approach to life, but not so with its architecture. Victorian architecture features an extravagant use of complex shapes, multitextured surfaces, multicolored walls, asymmetrical facades, steeply pitched roofs, and lots of doodads.

appearance of these structures rarely flaunted their progressive properties.

When it came time for the establishment to acknowledge these construction innovations, London's Great Exhibition of 1851, a world's fair aimed at the exaltation of scientific advancement, filled the bill. The revolutionary centerpiece building, which came to be known as the Crystal Palace, was designed not by a leading architect, nor even a brilliant engineer, but an English gardener, named Joseph Paxton. Instead of the stereotypical stone structure, the Crystal Palace was a network of iron columns, girders, and trusses bolted together and sheathed with 18,000 panes of glass. Regrettably, the building was destroyed by fire in 1936.

The Crystal Palace was made up of prefabricated components that were manufactured all over England and brought to the site for assembly. It was constructed in less than four months and represented a new concept in building technology.

FRENCH FLAIR AT THE FAIR

The immense popularity of London's 1851 Exhibition spurred other world expos. Paris outdid previous efforts with its Exhibition of 1889. The Machine Hall (demolished in 1910), a vast steel-and-glass creation, was a masterpiece of engineering. Gustave Eiffel (1832–1923) was hired to design an archway to mark the entrance to the fairground. He rose to the challenge and gave Paris the Eiffel Tower, which at the time of its construction was the world's tallest structure at 985 feet. A lot of conservative Parisians of the day thought the massive steel fabrication was an eyesore. Today, of course, it's the icon of the city.

The Eiffel Tower had no real purpose but what a grand gesture of frivolity.

AN OLD-FASHIONED FAIR ON THE LAKE

The London and Paris exhibitions played an important role in introducing bold new structural innovations to the masses. The Columbia Exposition of 1893 in Chicago was another equally pivotal event, but instead of embracing the new, this fair looked to the past. It was a major factor in an unprecedented revival of Neoclassical architecture in America. Basically, a bunch of rich white guys from New York set architecture back two thousand years. Reflecting the decidedly conservative mood of the country, the Columbia Exposition was heralded as a persuasive demonstration of how order, unity, elegance, and a vigorous allegiance to western European tradition could not only regenerate architecture but solve urban blight. As with other fairs, most of the buildings were temporary. However, Charles B. Atwood's Fine Arts Building was adapted to house Chicago's Museum of Science and Industry.

Around the same time, the New York firm McKim,

A BRIDGE GROWS IN BROOKLYN

The Brooklyn Bridge is a brilliant engineering creation that spans more than the East River. It is a fusion of art and engineering. Designed by J. A. and W. A. Roebling, the Brooklyn Bridge was the first wire suspension bridge and the longest suspension bridge in the world at the time of its completion in 1883. But the Brooklyn Bridge, like no other before it, allowed a person to experience riding or walking across a wide bay, high up in midair some 150 feet above the glittering waters.

Mead & White, who had taken part in the planning of the Chicago fair, really set the pace of the Neoclassical revival throughout the United States. In fact, they kept the style alive well into the twentieth century. Their Boston Public Library (1887–1893) is an elegantly detailed building, representative of grand civic structures of the late-nineteenth century, while their Villard Houses (1883–1885) in New York City, built of brownstone, are based on the palazzi of the High Renaissance.

Another major player in America's love affair with Neoclassicism was Richard Morris Hunt (1827–1895). He was the first American architect to be trained at the Ecole des Beaux-Arts in Paris, and he never forgot what he learned in school. When a *really* rich guy named George W. Vanderbilt hired him to design a summer home in the mountains of North Carolina, Hunt delivered an early-French Renaissance chateau called "Bilt-

With 255 rooms, Biltmore is one of the largest country houses.

HOMAGE TO A CATALONIAN

Decades before Frank Sinatra made famous the song "My Way," Catalonian architect Antonio Gaudi (1852–1926) was designing buildings in what can only be described as his way. He was *sui generis*; he didn't copy anybody and nobody copied him. In Barcelona, Gaudi's Church of the Sagrada Familia (1882, and still under construction) is more reminiscent of forms found in nature than of anything usually connected with serious architecture. When you look closely you can see birds, beetles, babies (which were actually cast from bodies in the mortuary), as well as lots of angels perched on knobs.

Gaudi's Sagrada Familia looks like the kind of castle you made by dripping wet sand at the beach, but it's actually built of stone and brick.

more." Hunt also designed a couple of beach houses for the Vanderbilts—the Breakers, an ostentatious neo-Renaissance palazzo, and the Marble House, both in Newport, Rhode Island.

ROMANESQUE REVIVED WITH GUSTO

Not all the historicist styles that were reclaimed were cutesy-cutesy or high art. Even much-maligned Romanesque architecture was ripe for a revival by the late 1800s. And nobody did it better than a brawny architect in Boston named Henry Hobson Richardson (1838–1886), or "H. H." to his friends. Architectural historians even named the popular style Richardsonian Romanesque in his honor.

Born in St. James Parish, Louisiana, Richardson graduated from Harvard and later studied at the Ecole des Beaux-Arts in Paris, probably the most influential architecture school ever. Richardson was the second American, after Richard Morris Hunt, to attend this Paris institution, but he didn't take his education as literally as Hunt.

Richardson set up a practice in New York in 1865 (not a lot of work back home after the war). Seven years later he relocated to Boston after he won a competition to design Trinity Church (1872–1877) on Copley Square. Just like the Romanesque originals, Richardsonian Romanesque buildings feature solid structures with round arches. But Richardson took a lot of interesting liberties. His buildings are usually built of rock-faced masonry with arches, lintels, deep window recesses, and details crafted of contrasting stone for emphasis. His large civic and commercial buildings feature multistory arched doorways and openings, as well as steep-gabled wall dormers. He loved to include square towers crowned with pyramidal roofs, large round turrets, and projecting bays. Chimneys are heavyset with little ornament.

Despite his obvious debt to a previous style, Richardson was a creative genius—one of America's truly great architects. His seven-story Marshall Field Warehouse in Chicago (1885–1887, and demolished in 1935) was a dramatic, load-bearing masonry building with mighty, round arches. It possessed elementary forms and an honesty of structure, greatly influencing later buildings and serving as a precursor of the whole Chicago School of Architecture (see Chapter 11).

Trinity Church (1874–1877) is dominated by a massive square central tower with round corner turrets.

SUMMARY

Nineteenth-century architecture was a period of "anything goes."

🕰 It was a hundred year cavalcade of revival with architects pulling more stylistic rabbits out of their top hats than we can count. Almost every architecture that had ever been had a "neo" prefix tacked onto it—neo-Gothic, neo-Romanesque, Neoclassical, neo-Greek, neo-Baroque, and neo-Renaissance—and was modified for the times.

🕰 The best buildings of the era were the work of great individualist architects who ran with the widespread revivalist traditions of the day but developed their own unique idioms.

🕰 The esthetic unity and cohesiveness of city streets were replaced by the cacophony of disparate buildings, each asserting its individuality.

🕰 The Industrial Revolution demanded new types of buildings for industry and transportation and concurrently offered new materials and construction techniques that made innovation possible.

🕰 Although many architects were slow to embrace changes in technologies, in the long run, the Industrial Revolution had more influence on architecture than all the design revivals put together.

CHAPTER 11

FOUNDATIONS OF MODERNISM

(1890–1920)

YOU MUST REMEMBER THIS

The seeds of an uprising against the historicism and rambling eclecticism of the 1800s were being sown by the turn of the twentieth century. Trends in the art community, including Cubism, Expressionism, Futurism, and Russian Constructivism, greatly influenced the shape of buildings. But even more important was the fact that architects first sought to reconcile the "singular artistic gesture" with the belief that a structure should above all else be designed to respond to its function.

MOST FAMOUS FOR

★ Wainwright Building, St. Louis, Missouri (1890–1891), Louis Sullivan
★ Glasgow School of Art, Scotland (1896–1909), Charles Rennie Mackintosh
★ AEG Turbine Factory, Berlin (1909), Peter Behrens
★ Einstein Tower, Potsdam, Germany (1919–1921), Erich Mendelsohn
★ Fallingwater, Bear Run, Pennsylvania (1935–1939), Frank Lloyd Wright

LAYING A FOUNDATION FOR
THINGS TO COME

As the nineteenth century was winding down, more and more architects were getting fed up with their entrapment within a web of historical precedents. A bold new architecture was rising in the United States. William Jenney's experimentation with steel-framed office buildings, combined with the widespread use of inventor Elisha Otis's electric elevator, allowed for taller and taller structures. In addition, rising land prices justified the added expense to build upward. This new building form, called the skyscraper, appeared in most major cities, but Chicago had the biggest and the best. And Louis Sullivan (1856–1924) built the creme of the crop. He not only mastered the technology, but he bedecked his structural marvels with uniquely conceived, free-flowing ornamentation. His Wainwright Building (1890–1891) in St. Louis, with its skeleton framework constructed entirely of steel, was a breakthrough in the evolution of the early skyscraper. Vertical members of the internal structural system are accentuated on the exterior of the building as massive brick piers. A deep, richly decorated frieze, accented with circular windows, crowns the top of the building.

The partnership of Daniel H. Burnham and J. W. Root also broke new ground with their Reliance Building (1890–1894), in Chicago. Originally designed as a four-story building, the Reliance grew to sixteen stories. The horizontal bands that mark the floors and the terra-cotta facing are the last echo of historicist ornament, while its fully developed skeleton construction allowed for large expanses of glass, not possible previously with other construction methods.

This new approach to commercial construction came to be known as the Chicago School. Buildings of the style were tall—usually six to twenty stories—in comparison to their predecessors. The new style's internal steel-framed skeleton allowed architects to use more and bigger windows. No longer was the exterior wall the structural support that actually held up the building. An internal steel frame structure was the real muscle. Claddings like terra-

The Wainwright is representative of Sullivan's distinctive low-relief ornament and intricately woven foliate patterns.

cotta, brick masonry, or other materials provided the exterior skin of the building. One of these new window treatments, which became known as the Chicago window, featured a large fixed central pane flanked by two narrow casements that opened for ventilation.

In the period from 1875 to 1900, there were incredible advances in terms of structure and personal architectural expression. The Chicago School style was the forerunner of the "glass skins" found on so many buildings today. Yet, the esthetic of the style—the restrained, straightforward exteriors—succumbed to the academicism of the Beaux-Arts movement (catapulted by those snobby East Coast guys who studied in Paris) and the popularity of the 1893 World's Columbia Exposition (see Chapter 10).

Building Your Architectural Vocabulary

Terra-cotta: Cast and fired clay units, usually more intricately detailed than bricks.

Skeleton construction: A way of building in which a steel frame or a structure of reinforced concrete carries all the weight of the structure.

Load-bearing construction: The walls actually hold up the building.

Oriel: A projecting window with its walls supported by brackets.

NEW BEGINNINGS IN THE OLD WORLD

In England, William Morris (1834–1896) pioneered the Arts and Crafts movement, an approach to architecture that called for capitalizing on the intrinsic beauty of materials and how they were used. He rallied against opulence and the tyranny of the machine and eschewed the Victorian practice of utilizing modern matter and methods simply to re-create the old less expensively. In rejecting academic conventions of the day, Morris and his followers turned to rural vernacular precedents for inspiration. Houses of the Arts and Crafts movement were crafted of no-nonsense materials and were deceptively simple and informal, with chimneys, rooflines, and windows providing the ornamentation.

On the Continent, Art Nouveau emerged as a loose grouping of romantic, decorative approaches that didn't have a direct connection with much of anything contemporary *or* historicist. The esthetic standards of Art Nouveau provided an effervescent atmosphere with writhing forms, flame-like lines, organically inspired details, and a deliberate simplification of structural elements. It didn't have a larger social purpose; the style was art for art's sake.

Belgian architect Victor Horta (1861–1947) was a leading proponent of the style. The grand staircase at his Hotel Tassel (1892) in Brussels is a forest of flowing iron curves, and his sinuous facade of the Maison du Peuple (1896 and demolished in 1965) was a deliberate departure from the building's carefully articulated structural framing. Hector Guimard (1867–1943) brought the style to Paris with a series of decorative entrances that still announce the city's Métro stations today.

"BEAM ME UP, SCOTTIE"

Scot artist and architect Charles Rennie Mackintosh (1868–1928) took the Art Nouveau style to new heights. His designs for Miss Cranston's chain of Glasgow tearooms show his penchant for decoration and elegant interiors, while his Glasgow School of Art (1896–1909) reflects his ability to deal with a larger structure—a disciplined design with only touches of frivolity. Elegant wrought-iron brackets adorn the large studio windows along the front facade.

However, in Austria and Germany these ideas really took off. One group of rabble-rousing artists broke away from the stuffy old Vienna Academy. With the catchy name, the "Secessionists," they espoused the need for an identifiable new architectural language. Others were

RELATIVE BUILDING FOR A RADICAL THEORY

Expressionist architect Erich Mendelsohn (1887–1953) designed the Einstein Tower in Potsdam, Germany (1919–1921) to house the famous scientist's astrophysics equipment, and he gave the building a bold, organic form. It still serves the purpose for which it was designed—proving that Mendelsohn was a master at reconciling the individual gesture with the demands of functionalism.

taking an even more radical approach. They didn't know it at the time but the seeds were being sown for Modernism. Theirs was an architecture of transition, bridging the gap between fashion and utilitarianism. Otto Wagner's Post Office Savings Bank (1904–1912) in Vienna is a massive structure with an exterior of marble slabs. But inside, the banking hall stands in light and airy contrast; its elegant curved ceiling is supported by slender concrete piers. The AEG Turbine Factory (1909) in Berlin, designed by Peter Behrens, is uncharacteristically noble for an industrial building. Its symmetrical design with an iron frame and barrel-vault roof embodies notions of simplicity, logic, and structural ingenuity.

ANOTHER ARTISTIC NOTION

The Dutch painter Piet Mondrian (1872–1944) developed an esthetic derived from Cubism and distinguished by primary colors, staggering geometrical forms, and smooth surfaces. A group of architects coined the term "De Stijl" and took Mondrian's concept to the third dimension. Gerrit Rietveld designed the landmark building of the style, the Schroder House (1924) in Utrecht. Apart from its rational planning, it is a playful composition of angular forms, interlocking planes, and colorful details.

THE WRIGHT STUFF

Frank Lloyd Wright (1867–1959) was the greatest American architect, according to himself and confirmed by a recent survey of the American Institute of Architects. In a career spanning more than seventy years, Wright produced hundreds of works, thousands of pages of writings, and seven children. He had also acquired three wives, numerous broken-hearted mistresses, and a cult-like following of former apprentices.

Wright learned the craft of architecture at the Chicago firm Adler & Sullivan, where he worked until 1893 when he started his own practice. And Sullivan was the only influence Wright ever acknowledged. He didn't waste any time making a name and style for himself. Within little more than a decade Wright created an impressive body of work and refined his Prairie Style of architecture, which featured low brick structures that hugged the expansive Midwestern landscape. Rather than designing one great building, Wright created scores of houses for his wealthy neighbors—business tycoons who were amassing fortunes in the railroads, industry, manufacturing, dry goods, and other respectable turn-of-the-century exploits. The best houses of this period include such landmarks as the 1902 Dana Residence in Springfield, Illinois, which represents Wright's early use of a two-story open living space; the 1904 Martin House in Buffalo, New York, one of Wright's largest Prairie Houses; and the 1906 Robie House, a dynamic low building with cantilevered roof eaves along a single-plane axis.

YOU CAN'T KEEP A GOOD MAN DOWN

The late 1920s and the Depression were hard on Wright. But the bad times didn't last. A department store magnate in Pittsburgh with deep pockets and a shallow creek allowed Wright at age 69 to revive his career. He firmly cemented his place in history, with a summer place named Fallingwater. Wright confidently extended free-floating platforms over a small waterfall and anchored the structure into the natural rock. Decidedly Modern with its interlocking geometries and engineering genius, the house is thoroughly fused with its site, in terms of form and materials. It was a manifestation of Wright's next approach to design (he hated the word "style"). He coined the term "organic architecture," which has nothing to do with not using fertilizer on the front lawn.

WRIGHT'S MASTERPIECES

Oak Park House and Studio, Oak Park, Illinois (1898–1895): It was his first home and office, but more importantly it was his early experimental laboratory where what would become hallmarks of his style first surfaced. It's now a museum.

Unity Temple, Oak Park, Illinois (1906): A radical departure from traditional liturgical architecture of the day, but what do you expect from a bunch of Unitarians?

The Robie House, Chicago (1906): This long, low structure is the most celebrated example of Wright's Prairie Style.

Johnson Wax, Racine, Wisconsin (1936–1947): A shin-

(*continued*)

ing example of the workplace of the future, it featured a curvy brick exterior and a vast office atrium held up by giant mushroom-stem columns.

Taliesin West, Scottsdale, Arizona (1938): It ain't no Graceland, but Wright does still have his groupies. As home to the Wright Foundation, Taliesin employs nearly a dozen full-time employees just to market and keep track of Wright trademarked drawings, furnishings, fabrics, and objects.

Fallingwater, Bear Run, Pennsylvania (1935–1939): Easy to remember, it's the house that cantilevers over a waterfall.

Fallingwater is Wright's brilliant integration of a house and the landscape.

WRIGHT'S FINAL CHAPTER

Wright was determined to exit this world in a blaze of glory. At age 85, he managed to get it up with gusto, creating a seventeen-story skyscraper for the Harold C. Price Company in Bartlesville, Oklahoma. Featuring cantilevered floors, zigzag vertical and horizontal detailing, and turquoise-colored accents, this idiosyncratic tower stood in sharp contrast to the sleek and shining corporate glass boxes soaring to new heights in New York City and Chicago in the early 1950s.

His next big erection came in the form of a unique synagogue, a sort of inverted colander, for Congregation Beth Salom in Elkins Park, outside of Philadelphia. And

---

DOCTORS BURY THEIR MISTAKES; ARCHITECTS CAN ONLY PLANT IVY

Marin County Civic Center (1957–1962): After sixty years of preaching that a building should be "of a hill not on it," Wright firmly set this building on not one but two hills, and filled in the valley between.

Hollyhock House (1916–1921): A dark and brooding Mayan fortress in Los Angeles, it was an iconoclastic detour. Even Wright supposedly said that "the damned thing will float away some day and be forgotten."

Annunciation Greek Orthodox Church (1956–1961): A glitzy flying saucer of a building by Wright, but maybe the fastest way to get to heaven from Wauwatosa, Wisconsin.

The Guggenheim's giant spiral ramp recalls a DNA strand.

last but certainly not least is the Guggenheim Museum, a spiraling mass of concrete. It's a grand example of architecture as sculpture, never mind the fact that it looks like a colassal flush toilet amid the staid facades of Manhattan's Fifth Avenue. The museum is a peculiar place to view art, but then it wasn't Wright who said "form follows function."

GONE BUT NOT FORGOTTEN: WRIGHTLY REMEMBERED

Larkin Company Building (1904): Underappreciated at the time, this elegant but boxy cathedral of commerce became a casualty to the post-World War II zeal to replace outmoded office buildings with parking lots.

(*continued*) . . . .

Midway Gardens (1915): Who says Disney was the first amusement park enterprise to hire "star" architects? This elaborate Chicago restaurant/casino took the "big fall" in the 1920s.

The Imperial Hotel (1915): East meets West in an ornate Byzantine maze that would do Conrad Hilton proud. It survived the great earthquake of 1923 and World War II, but succumbed to Tokyo's escalating land prices in the early 1960s.

Little House, Robinson Bay, Minnesota (1913): Actually a big house; the client's name just happened to be Francis W. Little. Still, the living room managed to fit nicely in the Metropolitan Museum of Art. It's there now.

We want to be, you know,
compatible with the environment.

Even discounting Wright's own hyperbole and his disciples' cult-like efforts to immortalize him, he was indeed a genius, an innovator, and in building matters, an eminently practical man. He was an experimenter, inventing or popularizing many new architectural devices. More importantly, he was in the vanguard in matters of design philosophy, challenging conventional wisdom on the shape, esthetics, organization and content of structure, and the role of architecture within a modern democratic society.

THE FOUNTAINHEAD: BIBLE OR BLASPHEMY

No book has shaped public opinion of architecture and those who practice it more than Ayn Rand's epic novel, *The Fountainhead.* Published in 1943, the compelling story of Howard Roark has lured more idealistic youngsters into the profession of architecture than a posse of guidance counselors and college recruiters.

Roark was depicted as being everything a young architect should be: brilliant, arrogant, selfish, iconoclastic, and invincible. His good looks were as unyielding as granite. Rand's characterization of Roark—the gifted young designer and his battle against the Donald Trumps of the day—was loosely modeled on Frank Lloyd Wright.

Rand argued that her treatise was a philosophical exercise and not a trashy novel about a sexy architect. Whatever, it's a page-turner filled with decidedly more action than *The Bridges of Madison County.*

SUMMARY

 The built environment fully reflected the effects of the Industrial Revolution.

The availability of steel framing, reinforced concrete, and plate glass challenged architects to use these materials in new ways. In Chicago, Louis Sullivan and others were the first to rise to the occasion, perfecting the skyscraper. The solidity of buildings could now be replaced by transparency thanks to stronger, thinner columns and cantilevers.

Not everybody embraced the idea of mass production and the advances of engineering. A reaction against industrialization resulted in the Arts and Crafts movement.

The Art Nouveau Movement emerged as a way to exploit the machine while celebrating the decorative possibilities of wrought iron, stained glass, and tile.

 Architects started questioning the relationship of form to function, laying the foundation for Modernism.

In this period of flux, America produced its greatest architect, Frank Lloyd Wright.

MODERNISM
(1920–1970)

YOU MUST REMEMBER THIS

All disguises of historicism and ornament were abandoned; the replacements were form and function, reason and abstraction. Not exactly the stuff that makes for buildings that are easy to love. You know the look of the style: sharp angles, concrete, steel, lots of windows (that usually don't open), white walls, flat roofs, barren plazas, and a barely distinguishable front door. The proponents of this new style believed that their architecture could change the world, and for the better. Their Utopia never quite materialized, but they did alter forever the appearance of cities and small towns around the globe.

MOST FAMOUS FOR

★ The Bauhaus, Dessau, Germany (1925–1926), Walter Gropius
★ PSFS Building, Philadelphia, Pennsylvania (1929–1932), Howe & Lescaze
★ Villa Savoie, Poissy, France (1929), Le Corbusier
★ Glass House, New Canaan, Connecticut (1949), Philip Johnson
★ Seagram Building, New York City (1954–1958), Mies van der Rohe
★ Salk Institute, La Jolla, California (1959–1965), Louis Kahn

UTOPIA, HERE WE COME

In the early years of the twentieth century, there was an architectural insurrection. The revolutionaries wanted a universal style that would be suitable for every occasion. The style would be called Modernism. Traditional design and historical precedents were declared null and void. Artificial symmetry was avoided at all costs, while balance and regularity were admired and fostered. Ornament, like the proverbial baby, was thrown out with the bathwater. The tripartite expression of base, middle, and top was heresy. Yet it was OK to expose mundane components such as mechanical equipment, structural members, and elevator shafts. Ribbon windows were a hallmark, as were corner windows, in which the glass was joined without interrupting supports.

The reformation started in Europe (didn't it always?), but many of its leading idealist designers soon relocated to the United States. Before they left the Continent they built some cool and restrained buildings that were deliberately understated. However, it was during the boom years following World War II that the style flourished and all the bad copies starting popping up faster than mushrooms after a spring rain.

But the trendsetting designers forgot that architectural fashion, like any other, thrives on change and variety. Nobody wants to wear the same outfit to the opera that is worn to the salt mines. So if "form follows function," it only follows that the form of an opera house shouldn't look like the form of a factory—or a fast-food restaurant, for that matter. Never mind that it takes a bit longer to erect a building than to adjust your hemline.

RUMBLINGS OF A NEW ORDER— AND I DON'T MEAN IONIC

The breeding ground for this bold new architecture was an arts school called the Bauhaus (translation: "to build" and "house"). German architect Walter Gropius (1883–1969) headed the school and designed a new facility when the school relocated to Dessau in 1922. Most regard it as his best building. During its heyday, it was *the* place to be, home to architects including Marcel Breuer and Mies van der Rohe (widely referred to by the single moniker Mies, kinda like Cher). Artists like Paul Klee, Wassily Kandinsky, Josef Albers, and Laszlo Moholy-Nagy also called it their house. More than a mere school, it was a lifestyle, a commune, and a radical, spiritual revelation—not exactly the kind of environment

SECOND PLACE IN THE SECOND CITY

In Chicago, styles were progressing, but a bit more slowly than in Deutschland. In 1922, the *Chicago Tribune* sponsored a competition for a new office tower. Several of the Bauhaus profs, as well as other leading European architects, submitted designs. An American, Raymond Hood, won the commission with a good old-fashioned Gothic-inspired extravaganza. Second place went to Finnish architect Eliel Saarinen (1873–1950). He didn't get the job, but he got a lot of good press for his futuristic scheme. (It was like everybody telling the runner-up that she's prettier than Miss America.)

It was one last hurrah for the old guard; after that, things would never be the same.

(continued) . . . .

The winner was really built.

with a bright future in Nazi Germany. Hitler shut down the place in 1933, and the avant-garde scattered, mostly to the United States, bringing their ideas with them.

A STYLE FOR ALL SEASONS

Meanwhile in Gotham City, specifically at New York City's Museum of Modern Art, a young whippersnapper

named Philip Johnson (b. 1906) and a slightly more serious architectural historian named Henry-Russell Hitch-
cock were mounting an exhibition that would prove
Modern architecture was actually a style with a precise
esthetic. The show was called "Modern Architecture: International Exhibition." It ran for less than six weeks in
1932, but more than sixty years later architects are still
debating its merits. It was either an extremely important
or an utterly dreadful development. Nine architects were
featured—Frank Lloyd Wright, Walter Gropius, Le Corbusier, J.J.P. Oud, Mies van der Rohe, Raymond M.

DESIGNS WITH A DIFFERENT AGENDA

By the time the Bauhaus had been shut down, most of
the talented architects had fled Nazi Germany. Modern
architecture and creativity had no place in the home of
the blitzkrieg: The Third Reich was much more interested in cultivating its own version of Neoclassicism
for its monumental buildings. One architect who never
considered leaving was Albert Speer (1905–1981). He
won most of the big Nazi commissions in the 1930s
and was eventually named Hitler's official state architect. His bombastic and authoritarian creations captured the mood of the country. Speer's designs for Hitler
included the 400,000-seat Nuremberg Stadium and Parade Grounds (1934) and the new Chancellery, or official residence (1938).

Speer was the only defendant at the Nuremberg war
crimes trials to admit his guilt, in his case the use of
slave labor. He served twenty years in Spandau prison,
where he wrote his memoirs, *Inside the Third Reich.*

Hood, Howe & Lescaze, Richard Neutra, and the Bowman Brothers (they faded into oblivion after the show)—with drawings of unbuilt projects, models, and photographs of actual buildings.

American cities became the proving ground for this radical new approach to design, which featured machine imagery, white walls, chrome, steel, and glass. Tagged the "International Style" after the MoMA exhibition, the label spread like wildfire. Ironically, today when Modernism is making a comeback, nobody wants to be associated with the "I" word.

Although many of the early large-scale projects in this genre never left the paper they were drawn on, the Philadelphia Savings Fund Society Building (1929–1932), designed by Howe & Lescaze and included in the show, made the important transition to glass and steel. There was no question that the PSFS Building looked "Modern," even though no one really knew what that meant.

COMING TO AMERICA

The architects featured in the MoMA exhibition went on to win fame and fortune. You already know about Wright, if you read the preceding chapter (but whatever you do, don't associate him with the International Style). The others were a little more open-minded to the label. Gropius landed at Harvard as head of the School of Architecture and went on to design an impressive slate of mediocre buildings in the United States. Topping the list is the Pan Am Building in New York City. It has a different name since Pan Am is kaput, but you know the one; it's the monstrosity that lurks beyond Grand Central Station. MetLife bought the Pan Am building in 1981 for a cool $400 million and changed the name immediately. Nobody said corporate icons come cheap.

Mies was named dean of Armour Institute, which was renamed Illinois Institute of Technology in Chicago. He was soon commissioned to design a whole new campus. His IIT master plan (1939–1940) called for a series of more or less similar buildings—glass-and-steel cages with an unabashedly industrial-strength stance, clustered

The City of Brotherly Love had never seen anything like the PSFS Building—a sleek and curving tower of glass and steel.

around a large, open superblock. The whole composition was carefully balanced, as if an auto assembly plant had been chopped into parts and set on the lawn in Charlottesville. His centerpiece was Crown Hall (1950–1956), which housed (surprise!) the School of Architecture.

Before Mies landed in the New Country in 1937, he had designed lots of buildings, but few actually got built. One that did was a small temporary building for a fair in Barcelona in 1929. You might have seen pictures of the Barcelona Pavilion with its dynamic interpenetrating planes of glass, honed green marble, travertine (another native Italian stone that looks great polished), and chrome-sheathed steel piers. They dismantled the structure but kept the chairs. You know the ones: criss-crossed steel, square seat and back. Re-creations of his Barcelona chair are still popular with people who want to appear hip.

Mies was not the typical academic type; he didn't like to write or discuss his buildings. He was the master builder. Let mere mortals talk about them. The high point of his career was his skyscrapers. The Seagram Building was his best—a dark, self-consciously sophisticated glass box the color of bourbon that rises above Park Avenue in New York City.

"IT'S MY PARTY, AND I'LL CRY IF I WANT TO"

It took nerve to build the first glass house, and Philip Johnson was the man for the job. In the late 1940s, Johnson was working for Mies, but that didn't preclude a little moonlighting. At the time, his boss was working on a transparent residence for the Farnsworths to be located in Plano, Illinois. Johnson beat Mies to the punch. In 1949, Johnson moved into his own Glass House in New Canaan, Connecticut. It was a rectangular Miesian steel-and-glass box interrupted only by the bathroom; it sits firmly on the ground.

SALIENT SLOGANS OF THE STYLE

Ornament is crime. Adolf Loos coined this witticism, though he never spelled out the penalties.

The plan is the generator. Le Corbusier maintained that the internal floor plan dictated the form of the building. It's a catchy saying but rarely true.

Form ever follows function. Louis Sullivan said it first, but Mies repeated it more often and dropped the "ever."

Less is more. Mies gets full credit for this one, but Robert Venturi upstaged him years later with "less is a bore."

God is in the details. Again, Mies. Should he have gone into advertising, or what?

Structure is the giver of light. Louis Kahn penned this one. Some still credit the sun.

Johnson lives in the Glass House. He shouldn't throw stones.

Mies's Farnsworth House was the more rigid, complex, and detailed of the two. It rests atop twelve thin steel white columns.

THE GREAT WHITE HOPE

Le Corbusier made the MoMA show, but remained in Paris, where he had worked since before the First World War. Born in Switzerland, he was christened Charles-Édouard Jeanneret, but everybody knows him by his self-appropriated pseudonym Le Corbusier, or the trendy Corbu. As a polemicist, Le Corbusier had no rivals (although Peter Eisenman is pushing it; see Chapter 14). His first book, *Vers une architecture,* articulated his philosophies and emphasized social issues, perhaps because there was no vocabulary in which to describe an esthetic that was still in the process of creation. But not to worry, he was working on that.

His early houses are Modern masterpieces. The Villa Savoie (1928–1930), located in Poissy, France, is the one to remember. Set on his trademark unadorned stick-like "pilotis" (whatever you do, don't call them columns—it's so bourgeois), the house features large open interior spaces and a sheer facade with ribbon windows all around, broken only at the corners.

Late in his career, Corbu softened up and every now and then he traded in his sharp geometries, thin planes, and plain pilotis for Rubenesque sculptural forms—thick walls and sensuous flowing shapes. The best of this genre is the Chapel at Ronchamp, France, which is more a sculpture than a building.

His theories on clustered housing were realized in L'Unite d'Habitation (1952) in Marseilles. The building is not quite as utopian in concrete as it was on paper. (Don't you hate it when that happens?) He finally got a commission to do a whole new city, Chandigarh, India.

Here Corbu explored theories that had been ruminating in his head for more than a half century. The Secretariat, the High Court, and the General Assembly Building comprise the monumental core. Time, as well as the climate, overcrowding, and civil strife, have been tough on these Modern icons. His only building in the United States is the Carpenter Center for the Visual Arts at Harvard (1960–1963).

GOOD GUYS FINNISH FIRST, IF ONLY IN THE INDEX

No discussion of Modern architecture would be complete without a mention of Alvar Aalto (1898–1976). Like most of his buddies, he dabbled in Neoclassicism before jumping on the Modern bandwagon. His best early works are in his native Finland, including a library at Viipuri (1936) and the unlikely candidate for design honors, a TB sanatorium at Paimio (1929–1933). Both these buildings were unassuming but quite humane, and maintained a sensitive harmony with the landscape. Aalto thrived in his homeland and developed an incredibly responsive approach to the region's long, dark, cold winters. He wasn't afraid of curving forms, warm textures, or soft surfaces, and his buildings are the most tactile and sensuous of the original Modernists. His later buildings include the Finlandia Concert Hall in Helsinki (1962–1973) and his Baker House at MIT in Cambridge, Massachusetts (1947–1948). Aalto also did some pretty innovative stuff with bent wood, including a popular chair that is still manufactured today.

Go West, Young Man

While other guys were espousing theory, Richard Neutra was building monuments to the International Style. A native of Vienna, Neutra worked briefly in Chicago for Holabird & Root and visited Wright at Taliesin before setting up shop in Los Angeles. Neutra was every bit as serious as his avant-garde contemporaries, but he managed to enliven the most severe abstractness with a dramatic ardor and sensitive handling of human needs. In other words, it would be fun to live in one of his houses. Southern California was perfect for Neutra, and vice versa.

Neutra mastered the relationship between indoors and outdoors. The classic photographs of his houses often show the wife and kids lounging poolside or on cantilevered decks. (Dad was working; this was a different era.) A Dr. Lovell commissioned Neutra to design a gleaming white house (1927–1929) perched on the hills of Los Angeles. Neutra's Modern parade of homes went on for years, up and down the Pacific Coast, not the least was the Tremaine House (1947–1948) near Santa Barbara. Neutra embodied creature comforts without a gabled roof or lace curtains, proving that a "home" doesn't have to look like a "house."

A few years earlier, the same Dr. Lovell had commissioned Rudolph Schindler, another Viennese émigré who settled in Los Angeles, to design a Beach House (1922–1926). It was supported on five concrete frames, allowing the beach to extend underneath the house to serve as a kind of outdoor living room. Two very big houses, both on great sites in Los Angeles, each by a prominent architect. Isn't that a tad excessive, Dr. Lovell? (He didn't have to worry about his earnings potential; health-care reform was unheard of.)

Los Angeles wanted to be the proving ground for innovative housing. *Arts and Architecture* magazine established a program called "The Case Study Houses" in the 1950s. Some really cool Modern houses were built—open plans, sliding doors, patios, and great views. They were supposed to be "affordable" and create a prototype for the contemporary American family. Of course, they did neither. Today, movie stars and the like live in them and they still look groovy—the houses, that is.

BUT THEY ALL LOOK ALIKE

The Modern house that had the *real* impact on how we live was not designed by a leading architect. Credit for that, as well as suburban sprawl and the erosion of the traditional American city, goes to a couple of tough New York Brothers, Fred and William Levitt, who developed the development. Their brainchild was a 800-square-foot two-bedroom cracker box in a place called Levittown. It began in 1947 on New York's Long Island and grew within four years to 17,000 nearly identical houses, each set on its own, albeit teensy, yard. Reviled by the architectural in-crowd, they were affordable "worker housing" that looked like houses in spite of their prefabricated components and assembly-line construction methods. The avant-garde wasn't impressed, but the swelling middle class that wanted to flee the city for the good life in the country gobbled them up. Eventually more than

120,000 houses were built in Levittowns in Pennsylvania, New Jersey, and Maryland.

GRAND GESTURE DOWN UNDER

The Sidney Opera House with its massive reinforced concrete shells cuts a bold, nautical profile in a harbor, but it wasn't always smooth sailing. Danish architect Jorn Utzon in association with London engineers Ove Arup & Partners won a competition in 1957 to design the building. Original estimates provided a five-year construction schedule and a $7-million budget. Sixteen years and $100 million later, Sidney had its Opera House. Some architects criticized the sail-like roofs as unfunctional and overtly romantic, patrons complained that there was no place to park, and Utzon had resigned halfway through construction after bitter in-fighting. But none of that seems to matter now: The building is an engaging sculptural addition to the Sidney waterfront and the icon of the city.

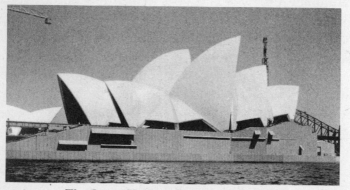

*The Opera House billows like sails above
its spectacular waterfront site.*

STANDING TALL IN THE CITY
WITH BIG SHOULDERS

Completed in 1974, the Sears Tower in Chicago is the tallest building in the world. It was designed by Skidmore, Owings & Merrill. With 110 stories and a height of 1,454 feet, the Sears Tower usurped Minoru Yamasaki's World Trade Center, which had held the title for barely a year. For the preceding forty years, the Empire State Building, designed by Shreve, Lamb and Harmon (1932), held the honor. The Empire State Building is a staggering engineering achievement, and its elegant glass-and-steel exterior and Art Deco form and detailing is an esthetic masterpiece. It is still by far the grandest American skyscraper. Only its petite sister, the Chrysler Building (1930) with its gleaming steel pinnacle, comes close.

The Empire State Building, right, is a building affair to remember.

The Chrysler Building, far right, with its fanciful Art Deco spire inspired by car parts, recalls the glory days of the automobile and still holds its own in the Manhattan skyline.

FAMILY TRADITION

Like the prodigal son, Eero Saarinen (1910–1961) rejected the architectural traditions of not only his dad, Eliel, but all the rest of the Modern establishment. Eliel, another talented Finnish émigré, designed some great craft-oriented buildings in Europe before coming to the United States in 1923. He settled outside of Detroit and designed a nifty campus for a school called Cranbrook in Bloomfield Hills (1924–1930). His Church of Christ (1939–1942) in Columbus, Indiana, is a Modern masterpiece, with a massive rectangular sanctuary of buff brick and limestone and a 166-foot-tall bell tower.

Eero soon tired of working in Dad's shadow and opened his own office in 1950. Eero always said that Modern architecture lacked drama, so he felt compelled to add some theatrics. He was that rare bird who never repeated a role; his buildings covered the gambit from Henry IV to Henry Higgins. His John Deere Administrative Center (1957–1964) was one of the first, and still one of the best, Modern suburban office buildings, and for a bunch of tractor executives, no less. He designed for them an intricate Miesian composition of an exposed steel structure, projecting sunscreens, and reflective glass windows.

Architecture purists like that building, but the people preferred his much more exciting role in St. Louis with the 630-foot-tall Jefferson National Expansion Memorial (1959–1964), or simply The Arch. Saarinen's goal was to create buildings with a memorable image, and most of his designs do just that. His TWA Building (1959–1962) at JFK Airport looks like a hawk or eagle in flight, while

Dulles Airport in Washington is more like a great blue heron with long concrete legs. Rounding off his design menagerie is the Ingalls Hockey Rink that looks a bit like a beached whale on the Yale campus.

He gave CBS a dark, brooding, unscalable fortress, fondly called Black Rock (1960–1964), on West 52nd Street in New York City, a building only Bill Paley could love. Proving again the old adage that only the good die young, Saarinen passed away suddenly in 1961, at the top of his game.

THEY HAD THEIR 15 MINUTES

Hey, you, get off my pedestal. The architectural media are every bit as fickle as a bunch of Hollywood gossip columnists. They love you, and then they leave you. Reputations that rise like a rocket can crash and burn just as abruptly. Paul Rudolph was one such golden boy. He was dean at Yale's School of Architecture when he was tapped to design the Art and Architecture Building in 1958. Ten years later the students set fire to the building in protest to its bunker-style ambiance.

Edward Durrell Stone was a star when he designed the Museum of Modern Art's new digs on 54th Street in Manhattan in the late 1930s. By the time he completed Washington's Kennedy Center for the Performing Arts, that immense marble box of carry-out pizza that sits along the Potomac, he was another victim of turns in fashion. At its dedication the building was met with a litany of ridicule, likening it to a "Soviet war memorial." Now at a quarter of a century, the Kennedy Center is

(*continued*) . . . .
accepted like any entertaining but overwrought and
aging "lady of the evening."

Canadians are also fair game. Moshe Safdie obtained
fame with his Habitat in 1967. Still believing technology
could solve urban problems, Safdie designed a prototype
modular housing project—his own version of worker
housing in the sky. Today it stands as a high-priced
condominium on the river's edge in Montreal. He was
just about to regain face when he proposed a twin-tow-
ered extravaganza for Columbus Circle that would have
cast a shadow halfway across Central Park. His scheme
was scrapped, as well as his comeback.

Arthur Erickson was British Columbia's rising star in
the 1960s. In the 1980s, he got the plum commission
to design the Canadian Embassy for a prominent site in
Washington, D.C. He fell flat on his face with a building
that straddles the stylistic fence between Modernism
and Classicism with as much finesse as a 400-pound
linebacker for the Canadian Football League.

TALK TO THE BRICKS

A bit like an architectural Dr. Doolittle, Louis Kahn
(1901–1974) was the Modernist who talked to his materials and told his students to ask, "What do you want,
brick?" But it was just that idiosyncratic approach to design, as well as his intellect, that made him so lovable.

Life was tough for Kahn. He survived impoverished
parents, a childhood accident that left him severely
scarred, bad hair, and thick glasses, only to succumb to
a heart attack in the men's room at New York's Penn

Station in 1974. History, however, is turning out to be much kinder to this Modern genius. In recent years there has been a renewed appreciation for Kahn's buildings, his style of teaching, and his romantic ramblings about architecture.

Kahn was a late bloomer. Although he was an influential teacher for decades, first at Yale and then at the University of Pennsylvania, he was nearly 60 before he came into his own as a "real" architect (i.e., one who builds buildings). His undisputed masterpiece is the Salk Institute in La Jolla, California. (Yes, the same Jonas Salk who discovered the vaccine for polio.) If you think Modern architecture isn't poetic, you haven't been to Salk. Kahn arranged the stark building on its rugged oceanfront site in a manner evocative of ancient Greek temples. You approach the building through a grove of

On a clear day you can see forever at Kahn's Salk Institute.

eucalyptus trees that opens onto a courtyard, which seems to reach to infinity. A controversial addition designed by some of Kahn's former students is underway.

His Kimbell Art Museum in Fort Worth, Texas (1966–1972) is a rare museum that succeeds as a work of art that doesn't take away from the pictures on the walls.

SUMMARY

 Modernism's roots were based in the industrial and architectural developments in Germany and Austria in the early years of the twentieth century.

 Ornamentation was out; puritanical asceticism was in.

 Stylistic consistencies were angular outlines, white walls, horizontal windows, flat roofs, stark plazas, no decorations, and lots of glass, steel, and concrete.

 More than a mere style, Modernism was a moral mission, out to change the world. But somewhere along the way the social idealism got lost in the esthetic shuffle.

 Love it or hate it, Modernism changed the look of cities all over the world.

CHAPTER 13

POSTMODERNISM
(1965–1989)

YOU MUST REMEMBER THIS

If Modernism with its stark structures is architectural anorexia then Postmodernism is bulimia. Inspired by Classical tradition and historical precedents, Postmodern architecture uses columns, pediments, porticoes, entablatures, symmetry, luscious materials, ornament, and peaked, pitched, and gabled roofs. For the first time in more than a generation, it was OK to make buildings witty, whimsical, colorful, and downright likable. Less was no longer more.

But at some point, too much was enough. By the end of a binge that lasted more than a decade, the world had been served up the architectural equivalent of everything from veal scallopini to Big Macs. Two-dimensional Greek temples were posing as strip malls, overscaled columns started popping up at home and the office, and every new corporate tower had a top that could entertain King Kong.

MOST FAMOUS FOR

★ Vanna Venturi House, Chestnut Hill, Pennsylvania (1961–1964), Robert Venturi

★ Neue Staatsgalerie, Stuttgart (1977–1983), James Stirling

★ AT&T Building, New York City (1978–1984), Philip Johnson, John Bugee

★ The Portland Municipal Services Building, Portland, Oregon (1980–1982), Michael Graves

THE STYLES, THEY ARE A-CHANGING

After a long and prosperous reign, Modern architecture fell out of favor with the avant-garde. It's not surprising. By the early 1960s, Modernism had become mainstream and the style of choice at practically every design school in the world. Its universal acceptance was also its undoing. The result was that around the world, not only buildings (and fast-food restaurants) but entire cities began to look alike.

The intellectuals of the profession couldn't embrace an esthetic that had such broad acceptance. They began the search for new design rationales. Proving that the pen is mightier than the sword (or sticks and stones in this case), Robert Venturi (b. 1925), struck a major blow to the movement with the 1966 publication of his "gentle manifesto," *Complexity and Contradiction in Architecture.* In his treatise Venturi espoused a series of rhetorical views that were opposed to those of traditional Modernism. He called for messy vitality rather than obvious unity, inclusion rather than exclusion, and ambiguity and complexity over straightforward simplicity. But architects can't live by words alone. He couldn't talk a real client into being his design guinea pig, so he built a house for Mother that actually did the things he was talking about.

The Vanna Venturi House (1962–1964) became an instant icon. The house, with its flat planar style and punched windows, was not totally inconsistent with Modernism but it was different enough to cause quite a stir. Venturi added molding details, oversized windows, and a central void with a broken arch and pediment to mark

the front door. In addition, the scale was deliberately
distorted and the pitched roof represented a romantic
version of "home."

Venturi also professed a love of the "ugly and ordinary." These ideas were taken up in his Guild House
(1963–1966), a mid-rise apartment building for the el-
derly. The building's facade of red brick is like the rest
of the nearby houses in this working-class neighborhood
in Philadelphia. The thin cheap-looking double-hung
windows are standard but oversized and distorted in
shape. Adorning the roof is a nonfunctioning television
in gold anodized aluminum. With these two buildings,
Venturi turned the commonplace into the uncommon
through amplification and shifts in scale, in much the
same way that Pop artists like Andy Warhol transposed
a banal object like a Campbell's soup can into a work
of art.

But like most rebellious children, Venturi mellowed.
He started designing respectable, but slightly funky,

*Venturi's house for his mother: This Vanna never
twirled any letters, but her house still turns heads.*

WHAT'S IN A NAME?

A new style has to have a new name. "Postmodern" was the label given to the architectural movement. (Others used the word first, but an Anglophile named Charles Jencks usually gets the credit for coining the term, basically because he sold a lot of books on the subject.) Yet Postmodernism lacks the development of a cohesive architectural style. It emerged as a loose characterization for many fragmented efforts, primarily concerned with historical styles, contextualism, symbolism, and ornament. Although these efforts contributed to a reexamination of architectural form, they didn't generate any truly original designs.

buildings for colleges and museums. In 1986 he was tapped to design an addition to London's National Gallery. His Neoclassically inspired Sainsbury Wing, completed in 1991, stands unobtrusively beside its historic predecessor and keeps its mouth shut. Venturi really didn't have much choice. His scheme came after Prince Charles had called an earlier, and unabashedly Modern, proposal by another architect a "monstrous carbuncle on the face of a much-loved and elegant friend."

AN ARCHITECT WITH A
SENSE OF HUMOR

In the meantime, Charles Moore (1925–1993) was advocating a more humanistic and playful approach to design, without the snobbish academics. He was one of the first architects to take the pedestrian scale, imagery, and urbanism (albeit contrived) of America's theme parks seriously, acknowledging their place, humor, and contributions to America's pop culture. Moore also designed environmentally sensitive buildings years before the first Earth Day. In 1965, in association with Moore Lyndon Turnbull & Whitaker (the first of seven firms he co-founded), Moore designed Sea Ranch Condominium on a 5,000-acre former sheep ranch along the Pacific Coast a hundred miles north of San Francisco. Inspired by regional precedents, topography, and the climate, rather

THE TELLTALE SIGNS OF A POSTMODERN BUILDING

Can the building be described as cute, whimsical, or playful?

Does it have a big front door?

Does it have a recognizable base, middle, and top?

Does the top look like a hat, piece of furniture, pyramid, ziggurat, a small animal, or rigging for a dirigible?

Does the ornament appear to be pasted on the facade, as if all its exterior doodads were an afterthought?

Are there a lot of big fat columns that don't support anything substantial? Or skinny silver palm-tree columns that don't support anything?

Are the interiors painted colors that should be reserved for bridesmaids' dresses?

than the dictates of Modernism, the original Sea Ranch comprised a grouping of ten apartments, each basically a 24-foot cube. The buildings featured varied shed roofs that merged politely with their rugged landscape, and their post-and-beam construction and cedar siding recalled barns rather than your typical oceanfront vacation house.

While others were talking about making architecture more inclusive, Moore did something that was unheard of. He staged town meetings and invited the people who would actually use the structures to express their opinions about everything from churches to city halls to museums.

SOMETHING OLD, SOMETHING NEW, SOMETHING BORROWED, SOMETHING BLUE

During the 1970s the fledging Postmodern movement spawned a lot of exquisite Classical and colorful drawings, as well as a few real apartments, houses, showrooms, and boutiques. By the decadent decade of the 1980s, Po-Mo hit the big time. After the dedication of the Portland (Oregon) Public Service Building, things would never be quite the same. Three years earlier, Michael Graves had won a controversial competition to design the building, and with the commission he delivered the first monument of the style. The Portland Building pays homage to a variety of traditional precedents: it has a clearly articulated base, middle, and top; the ground floor is enclosed by a sheltering loggia; exterior wall surfaces are mostly ceramic tiles and painted concrete surfaces; and side elevations boast stylized garlands that impart its "gift-wrapped" imagery.

Love it or hate it, the Portland Building made Graves a star. A year later, a small public library in San Juan Capistrano showed he had some talent. The library's plan recalls a cloistered monastery, and its forms are clearly Gravesian with a decidedly Californian twist. The composition is an idiosyncratic synthesis, but perfect for a town known for a famous Spanish mission, as well as the legendary returning swallows. Graves broke the building into a series of small-scale stucco structures

The Portland Building puts billboard Classicism on permanent display.

AN OLD DOG TURNS A NEW TRICK
. . . .
Usually only whiz kids have the energy for a new style, but ever-young-at-heart Philip Johnson (see Chapter 12) rallied to the cause and convinced corporate America that Postmodernism was the only way to go. Located in midtown Manhattan, his AT&T Building is clad in pink granite and rises thirty-seven stories to its famous top— a massive split pediment—indisputably the world's largest Chippendale highboy.

---

crowned with red clay tiles, and incorporated colonnades and landscaped courtyards.

A master plunderer of architecture's sourcebooks, Graves isn't bashful about quoting Roman, Greek, Tuscan, Egyptian, Art Deco, Constructivist, and Cubist references. He can be as serious as a heart attack when his client is Humana, the giant health-care provider. For them he delivered a monumental, polychromatic, sculpted twenty-five-story headquarters building (1982–1985) in Louisville, Kentucky. On a less serious note, for Walt Disney's Burbank headquarters (1989–1991), Graves uses seven 19-foot-tall dwarfs to support a vaguely Neoclassical pediment and paired barrel-vaulted rooflines that resemble Mickey's ears.

THE ARCHITECT JAY GATSBY WOULD HIRE

While other architects were only flirting with romantic tradition, Robert A.M. Stern fell head over heels for historical precedent. He built a series of big beach houses for rich Northeasterners—gracious Shingle Style houses, unobtrusive yet monumental, with gracious front porches and interior spaces that flow like the sea breeze. His pitched roofs, wooden surfaces, verandas, gables, dormers, and eyebrow windows could make Martha Stewart feel right at home. This was an architectural vocabulary everybody could understand, if only a few could afford. Inside, the houses are filled with architectural ornamentation—crown molding, chair rails, inlaid wood, window niches, and anything else that could be construed as old-fashioned. His houses gave new sanctity to "rooms" after

PITHY PLATITUDES OF POSTMODERNISM

All styles are good except the boring kind. Voltaire said it in 1736 to encourage diversity and multiculturalism. The proponents of Postmodernism were glad to embrace all kinds of styles, 240 years later.

Main Street is almost all right. Robert Venturi called for architectural snobs to appreciate old-fashioned aspects of design and planning that have worked for hundreds of years. He found inspiration in such mundane places as a small town's Main Street (as well as Las Vegas). However, he couldn't explain why they always build the Wal-Mart on the outskirts of town in a strip mall.

You cannot not know history. Philip Johnson called for young architects to go study and make the architecture of the past. If you believe him, he has always known everything.

years of "space," praised the processional route of corridors, and glorified the ceremony of entry.

DESIGNS FARTHER AFIELD

European architects such as Aldo Rossi (b. 1931) and James Stirling (1926–1992) were also seeking to transcend Modernism while harking back to a broader architectural language. In Italy, Rossi stripped his buildings down to the fundamentals and used the most elementary of Classical forms. His "House of the Dead" cemetery at Modena, Italy (1971–1984), comprises simple, linear wings with pitched roofs, colonnades with flat concrete piers, and repetitive square four-pane windows. He'd also branched out, geographically as well as esthetically. His Hotel II Palazzo in Fukuoka City, Japan (1987–1989) combined a weird contemporary version of wood construction, repetitive, unadorned columns, and overscaled green steel beams that mark the floors.

ARCHITECTURE FOR ART'S SAKE

If museums have taken the place of the churches in our culture, as Philip Johnson maintains, then the commission of a lifetime for a contemporary architect is a building devoted to the arts, not the gods. So no St. Paul's for British architect James Stirling (1926–1992); his masterpiece is Neue Staatsgalerie in Stuttgart, Germany. The museum is an energetic collage of unusual forms and bright colors set atop a modern-day Acropolis (actually

*Neue Staatsgalerie is a bustling urbanistic
and artistic success.*

a parking garage). The facades are a variegated pattern
of sandstone, travertine, and concrete. Hot pink and
bright blue railings and serpentine glass walls framed in
green provide more than a hint of color. The center of
the building is a circular outdoor sculpture court, a piazza or a rotunda complete with a "domeless dome."
Stirling acknowledged affinities to the ruins of Hadrian's
Villa, while his critics likened the scheme to the Fascist
Classicism of Albert Speer.

Back in London, Stirling's addition to the Tate Gallery
(1982–1986) is even more colorful and eccentric than
his German expression. Like a chameleon, the building

has a variety of exterior surfaces that reflect different interior functions and respond to the diverse original buildings of the complex.

A PICTURE-PERFECT PATCH OF POSTMODERNISM

In addition to a call for traditional building forms, architects were rallying for a return to old-fashioned town planning. A couple of brothers named Robert and Leon Krier started the movement in Europe. But a Miami husband-and-wife team, Andres Duaney and Elizabeth Plater-Zyberk, actually built one on a little plot of land facing the Gulf of Mexico in a section of Florida called the "Redneck Riviera." Named Seaside (1982), the planned "new town" is the cutest collection of people-size dollhouses you could possibly imagine. Strict zoning and guidelines generate gingerbread houses, picket fences, sidewalks, front porches, but most of all, nostalgia for small-town America.

At Seaside, they managed to turn the clock back to a time that never existed.

SUCCESSFUL TRIOS

Even mainstream Modernist firms jumped on the Po-Mo bandwagon in the 1980s, if only temporarily. Skidmore, Owings & Merrill, once called "the three blind Mies," started dabbling with decoration. Founded in Chicago in 1936, SOM (initials are big with architecture firms, unlike law firms where you must spit out all of the partners' names) rose to prominence in post-war America, employing as many as 2,500 architects at its peak. They designed sleek commercial structures, from Lever House on Park Avenue (it's the green glass box across the street from Mies's brown glass box for Seagram) to International Style banking towers for Arab oil sheiks to the concrete donut known as the Hirshhorn Museum in Washington, D.C. Their Postmodern contributions in-

Procter & Gamble was inspired by Art Deco and early European Modernism. Its massing with two low wings angled to rise as a pair of towers was a novel solution that appropriately responded to its urban site.

clude Rowes Wharf (1986–1989) in Boston, Worldwide Plaza in Manhattan, and AT&T in Chicago.

But the trio that captured the hearts and pocketbooks of commercial clients in the 1980s was undoubtedly Kohn Pedersen Fox. Their Procter & Gamble headquarters in Cincinnati, Ohio (1983–1985) is a majestic ensemble with elegantly detailed twin towers that elevated commercial architecture to new heights. By the close of the 1980s, KPF had designed historicist towers from Charlotte, North Carolina, to Seattle to London, and almost every major city in between. But fashions, like the tides, always turn.

PO-MO'S POSTMORTEM

By the early 1990s, finding an architect who called himself or herself a Postmodernist was as difficult as that proverbial camel passing through the eye of a needle. The proponents of Postmodernism marked the death of Modernism on July 15, 1972, when the city of St. Louis dynamited Pruitt-Igoe, a housing project completed less than twenty years earlier in the heady days when people actually believed architecture could change lives.

ON THE FIRST DAY, GOD SUB-CONTRACTED

THE ATLANTIC | THE PACIFIC | THE INDIAN | THE ARCTIC

McKIM, MEAD & WHITE   I.M. PEI   SKIDMORE, OWINGS & MERRILL   EERO SAARINEN

CRAWFORD

Pruitt-Igoe was designed by Minoru Yamasaki (architect of New York's World Trade Center), and it actually won some prestigious architectural awards. The high-rise concrete apartment block was, needless to say, a dismal failure. If it did change lives, it was only for the worse.

Following that logic, the detonation of EuroDisney would be the perfect epilogue to Postmodernism. We can only wish upon a star.

SUMMARY

 Feeling bored and boxed in, Postmodern architects looked to the past for inspiration for the future.

 The movement delivered a much-needed dose of humanism and spawned some memorable buildings.

 At its best, Postmodernism allowed designers to talk about issues like humanism, historicism, contextualism, and regionalism, while incorporating indigenous materials, vernacular forms, and traditional precedents.

 At its worst, the Postmodern movement was a literal reading of historical quotes and allusions that were so simplistic they were clichés, or so esoteric that they became unintelligible.

 But if "architecture is frozen music" as Goethe said, then the worst examples of Postmodern architecture must be "frozen Muzak."

CHAPTER 14

CONTEMPORARY PLURALISM

YOU MUST REMEMBER THIS

Architecture in the latter part of the twentieth century is in an esthetic flux that borders on design anarchy. Unlike the mid-twentieth century with its litany of *isms,* from Modernism to Postmodernism to Regionalism to Deconstructivism to Neo-modernism, leading architects now shun stylistic labels with a vengeance. An architect today doesn't want to be associated with a movement, unless it's a style associated with his or her own unique approach to design.

MOST FAMOUS FOR

★ East Wing, National Gallery of Art, Washington, D.C. (1972–1978), I. M. Pei & Partners

★ Gehry House, Santa Monica, California (1976–1979), Frank O. Gehry & Associates

★ Vietnam Veterans Memorial, Washington, D.C. (1982), Maya Lin

★ Wexner Center for Art, Columbus, Ohio (1986–1989), Peter Eisenman

★ J. Paul Getty Museum, Los Angeles (1988–?), Richard Meier & Partners

VIRTUAL REALITY OR REAL VIRTUES?

Late-twentieth-century architecture seems to lack the stylistic single-mindedness of other periods in history. Perhaps this is because when we study periods of the more distant past, their lesser buildings fall by the wayside and only the strong survive. But even allowing for that, the current scene is muddled with all kinds of design directions. By all accounts, the present state of architecture has no clear bearings. The concept of a universal style has lost credibility, and there is no sense of where or from what a style might emerge.

Today there might not be an internationally accepted movement, but every generation sends a hero up the pop charts, as the Paul Simon song goes. And the design profession is no exception. Some architects have illustrious careers that have spanned decades and have weathered the winds of fashion, while others are one-hit wonders who burst onto the scene with a single sensational structure. I. M. Pei is the Frank Sinatra of design, with a consistent and predictable repertoire of memorable, albeit Modern, numbers. Frank O. Gehry, with his growing portfolio of hard-hitting compositions, is more akin to Bruce Springsteen or a progressive rock group like R.E.M., while Peter Eisenman, with his flock of undiscerning groupies, is closer to The Grateful Dead.

IF IT AIN'T BROKE, DON'T FIX IT

To paraphrase Mark Twain, reports of the death of Modernism are greatly exaggerated. It's more like the

UNMONUMENTAL MONUMENT

Maya Lin was a 21-year-old architecture student at Yale University when she won a national competition with a design for a memorial to honor veterans of the Vietnam War. At the initial unveiling of the scheme, some die-hard patriots worried that an angled 440-foot-long retaining wall, inscribed with the names of the American men and women killed or listed as missing in action, was not dramatic enough. They couldn't have been more wrong. The memorial was dedicated on Veteran's Day in 1982, and it is one of the most emotive structures of contemporary architecture. In addition, it has become one of the most-visited spots in Washington, D.C.

The Vietnam Veterans Memorial is a slab of black granite set into the ground and has served as a new model for monuments around the world.

Eveready bunny: the style keeps going and going and going—with about as many turns as that ubiquitous rabbit. And nobody does it better than I. M. Pei (that's short for Ieoh Ming, but please call him I. M.).

Born in China in 1917, Pei came to the United States to study in 1935 and didn't look back. In 1978, when most leading architects had abandoned the supposedly sinking Modernist ship, Pei's East Wing of the National Gallery in Washington, D.C., opened to rave reviews from the public and the design profession. It was a totally abstract composition of interlocking triangles crafted of marble. It's the most adventurous, most sculptural, and most successful piece of Modern architecture in the Capital.

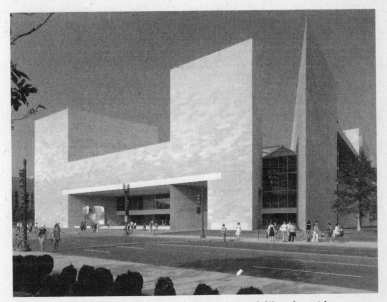

Pei's East Wing is a self-proclaimed liberal amid a bunch of stuffy old conservatives.

Throughout the 1980s, Pei stuck with a good thing and went on to design bold buildings ranging from the seventy-story Bank of Hong Kong with a dramatic X-bracing pattern on the facade to the cool and abstract Creative Artist Agency in Los Angeles. Pei's thriving practice has designed almost every kind of building imaginable, including hospitals like Mt. Sinai's Guggenheim Pavilion on Fifth Avenue, convention centers in New York and Los Angeles, museums, symphony halls, corporate towers, and even the Rock and Roll Hall of Fame in Cleveland, Ohio.

IT'S AN OLD MAN'S PROFESSION

Young lawyers complain that it takes seven or eight years to be named a partner. Pity the poor architects. Look at James Ingo Freed and Henry N. Cobb—not exactly a couple of underachievers. They rate as two of the most talented designers of the past thirty years. Freed recently completed the Holocaust Memorial Museum in Washington, D.C., and Cobb was the architect of Boston's Hancock Tower and served as chair of the Harvard Graduate School of Design from 1980 to 1985. Cobb was 64 and Freed was 59 when they finally got their names on the front door of the office. In 1989, I. M. Pei & Partners became Pei Cobb Freed & Partners.

OFF THE BEATEN TRACK

Most architects allege that they aren't affected by the winds of fashion; 99 percent of them are lying. A very select few actually follow their hearts when it comes to

design. E. Fay Jones is one. He's also humble, which is
an even rarer characteristic. (Architects from the beginning of time have been notorious for their monumental
egos.) Jones was born in Pine Bluff, Arkansas, in 1921,
and has practiced in the state most of his life. His portfolio is filled with small-scale churches and houses that
fit the rolling landscape of the rural South as comfortably as a pair of old shoes. Jones studied briefly under
Wright, but he hasn't slavishly copied the master. Jones
has combined Wright's theories (on integrating a building with the environment) with historic models and local

*Thorncrown reverses Gothic construction: the building
is pulled together by light interior wood members in tension
rather than being pushed together from the outside by
massive stone supports.*

building traditions (also known as "vernacular") to create his own vocabulary with a decidedly Southern drawl. His most famous building is Thorncrown Chapel, a modest pilgrimage shrine in the woods near Eureka Springs, Arkansas. Using the sparest of means, Jones crafted the building as a delicate web of wooden trusses rising above a low base of native fieldstone. His Pinecote Pavilion (1988) in Mississippi is a simple structure for gatherings and presentations at a nature preserve. It couldn't be less obtrusive.

EAST MEETS WEST

Japanese architecture, with the exception of vernacular houses, has pretty much always been dominated from abroad, first by Chinese techniques and later by traditional western European influences. It wasn't until the 1950s and 1960s that Japan created its first uniquely national approach to design. The movement is known as Metabolism, which holds that architecture should not be static but be capable of undergoing metabolic changes. Instead of thinking about issues of form and function, architects should address space and changeable uses. The granddaddy of the approach is Kenzo Tange (b. 1913); the younger followers included Fumihiko Maki (b. 1928), Kisho Kurokawa (b. 1934), and Arata Isozaki (b. 1931). The post-war reorganization of the Japanese government and booming economy provided lots of opportunities for this Eastern brand of Modernism to blossom. To Japanese architects, the 1964 Olympics in Tokyo represented a chance to show the rest of the world what they were up to. Tokyo architect Kenzo Tange's pair of Sports Halls was a bold structural composition. The bigger of the two structures features the largest suspended roof in the world—a welded steel net slung from two reinforced concrete masts.

By the 1970s, however, Japanese architects like Isozaki were looking toward more traditional historical references and purer forms. His Gunma Prefectural Museum of Fine Arts (1974) demonstrates the developing interplay between East and West. Isozaki also found an audience in the United States. He designed the Los Angeles Museum of Contemporary Art and the Team Disney Building (1990) in Orlando, Florida.

THE GREAT WHITE WAY

Other architects like Richard Meier never stray from the dictums of old-fashioned Modernism (or at least Meier hasn't yet). All his buildings are cool, white, precise, intellectual, elegant, and crafted of porcelain-enameled-steel panels. But what's wrong with perfecting a consistent theme?

Meier has designed scores of structures, including houses, cultural institutions, office buildings, and museums that all look remarkably similar. Starting in the 1990s, he began using, if ever so cautiously, accents of stone and masonry; he promised something new and different for his J. Paul Getty Museum, which should open before the year 2000, but the scheme looks remarkably like a Meier building, just a *lot* bigger.

Granted, Modernism might have suffered the architec-

The High Museum in Atlanta (1983) is typical
of Meier's unflagging esthetic.

tural equivalent of an out-of-body experience during the
1980s, but the light at the end of the tunnel was probably
a gleaming white edifice by Meier that would make Le
Corbusier proud.

GEHRY GROWS UP

Living in southern California does something to you—
and that goes for architects as well as surfers. Canadian-
born Frank O. Gehry has spent nearly five decades in
America's great illusionistic metropolis, Los Angeles. In

that time, he invented an architecture that captures the spirit of the place and then found a worldwide market for it.

Gehry rejected the obvious romanticism that epitomizes southern California and embraced the banal to create poetic compositions in his own idiom. Fifteen years ago, his schemes were wildly controversial. One local architecture critic called him a "madman with a two-by-four."

An early pivotal building was his own home, which he described as a "dumb little house with charm" in a nice Santa Monica residential neighborhood. In what can only be described as a *radical* remodeling, Gehry sur-

Gehry has gone on to design bigger and better buildings, but his funky little house said it first.

rounded the modest house with a screen of plywood, chain-link fencing, corrugated aluminum siding, and other previously unglamorous materials. Inside, he stripped away the old finishes of the house to expose the studs of the original walls.

Gehry took his southern California approach around the world, first with houses and relatively small institutional projects. But by the late 1980s, Gehry hit the big time with such diverse projects as Vitra's swirling furniture factory and museum in Germany, a schizophrenic-looking psychiatric Institute at Yale University, and a fishy restaurant in Kobe, Japan, that literally looks like a giant carp, with scales and all.

In 1994 his American Center in Paris won the hearts of the cynical French population—and it takes a lot of effort by any American to get a rise out of Parisians. Planned as the cultural centerpiece of a redeveloped district overlooking the Parc de Bercy, the 198,000-square-foot center is characteristic of Gehry's evolving esthetic ideology with its assemblage of disparate forms and curvilinear ribbons of limestone and metal. And it shows that with a big budget, he doesn't disappoint.

Not everybody in Los Angeles immediately loved his approach, but lots of young architects around town ate it up. They found inspiration in Gehry's combination of roughhouse informality and intellectual clarity. He is an original in his use of common materials in unexpected ways, his idea of a building as a collage, his conglomeration of sculptural forms, and his unpretentious yet highly artistic ambitions. A band of loyal followers picked up on the methods, established offices, and built scores of houses and chic restaurants in the oceanfront communities of Venice and Santa Monica. And a few firms, like Morphosis, Eric Owen Moss, and Rebecca Binder, have actually taken the Gehry esthetic and some interesting buildings with their own twists.

BACK TO THE FUTURISM: THE STYLE THAT CAME AND WENT FASTER THAN THE SHOW

In 1988, MoMA mounted an architectural exhibition about a possible new style called "Deconstructivist Architecture." The pre-show hype promised an event to rival the 1932 International Style exhibition that had helped usher in Modernism (see Chapter 12). The museum even hired Johnson again; he did such a good job fifty-seven years earlier.

The term Deconstructivism came from a bastardization of the Russian Constructivist movement of the 1920s and the idea of deconstructing a building. The style was obsessed with diagonals, arcs, warped planes, skewed volumes, and irregular angles. Seven architects participated: Peter Eisenman, Frank Gehry, Zaha Hadid, Rem Koolhaas, Daniel Libeskind, Bernard Tschumi, and the firm Coop Himmelblau. This was a group that bragged about how they had replaced the traditional design virtues of harmony, unity, and clarity with disharmony, fracturing, and mystery. It was little more than nostalgia for the early-twentieth-century avant-garde.

The show turned out to be the architectural equivalent of the emperor's new clothes. The idea of a contrived universal style had no merit, and the appeal of the show was over before the monthly magazines had time to print their reviews.

But some of the crazy schemes were actually built. In 1989, when the Wexner Center for the Visual Arts at Ohio State University by Peter Eisenman was dedicated with great fanfare, "style" had become a dirty five-letter word rarely used by the enlightened. So nobody dared place it in a stylistic category. The Wexner is a convoluted scheme of weird angles and layers of crazy geometric patterns and esoteric allusions. Eisenman claims the building is aligned with the university's football stadium and on the "Mercator grid" (whatever that is) and claims it should be understood as "critiques of humanism and anthropocentrism." Most visitors to the center are happy if they can find the bathroom.

If God is in the details, the Wexner Center is a design high holiday. But for this architectural agnostic, a little bit less would have been more.

ANY *ISM* GOES

It is cliché to say that the current architectural scene is pluralistic and eclectic and that the ideological future of the profession is up for grabs. Like most clichés, it's basically true, but it's a relatively unsatisfying analysis of the situation.

The good news is that it's cool to like any style of architecture. But don't waste your time looking aimlessly at all the unimportant stuff that stands in most cities. You should concentrate on those structures that rise above the ordinary. In addition, you shouldn't be afraid of expressing a fondness for some off-beat brand of design. In fact, the more esoteric your choice of style, the more likely you will be to impress your friends.

SUMMARY

⏱ Contemporary architecture is a pluralistic state of affairs with no single universal style or clear direction of where it's headed.

⏱ Diverse reinterpretations of tradition continue to flourish, and the heroism and abstraction of Modernism still attracts a loyal following.

⏱ Within this environment of architectural laissez-faire, a number of talented architects have developed their own highly personal signature styles, from the exuberant romanticism of Frank Gehry to the restrained rationalism of Richard Meier to the down-home craftsmanship of Fay Jones.

Style is a bad word. But any architect would more than gladly align with a namesake "style" of his or her own making, which would assure a prominent place in the design history books. (Buildings can be torn down, but a style is forever.)

The disorganized state of design is not peculiar to the end of the twentieth century. In the final days of the nineteenth century as now, the world witnessed the widespread revival of a variety of past styles and a wave of exotic eclecticism.

Perhaps the time is ripe for someone with a sense of architectural history—maybe you—to give the world the new style it claims not to be waiting for.

ABOUT THE
AUTHOR

ELEANOR LYNN NESMITH writes about design for *Southern Living* magazine. She is a former senior editor of *Architecture* magazine and the author of *Health Care Architecture: Designs for the Future.* She has also written articles for *Architectural Record, Inform, Southern Accents, Washingtonian* and *The Washington Post Magazine.* She is a graduate of the University of North Carolina, Chapel Hill, and lives in Birmingham, Alabama.